WHY
THE RAMONES
MATTER

Music
Matters

Evelyn McDonnell
Loyola Marymount University
Series Editor

WHY THE RAMONES MATTER

Donna Gaines

UNIVERSITY OF TEXAS PRESS
AUSTIN

Requests for permission to reproduce material from this work should be sent to:

    Permissions
    University of Texas Press
    P.O. Box 7819
    Austin, TX 78713-7819
    utpress.utexas.edu/rp-form

♾ The paper used in this book meets the minimum requirements of ANSI/NISO Z39.48-1992 (R1997) (Permanence of Paper).

Library of Congress Cataloging-in-Publication Data available upon request
ISBN 978-1-4773-1871-3 (cloth: alk. paper)
ISBN 978-1-4773-1875-1 (library e-book)
ISBN 978-1-4773-1873-7 (nonlibrary e-book)

doi:10.7560/318713

For the
Greater Glory of God,
the Ramones,
and the
Generations Rising

....

CONTENTS

....

PREFACE

....

The Ramones are my band. Over the years every song has been for me. Why else would they have written "53rd & 3rd," about my former subway stop; or valorized glue, my favorite high school drug; or, in the highest-charting original song of their career, canonized my birthplace, Rockaway Beach? On top of that, perfectly predicting my career trajectory—a teenage lobotomy-cum-PhD.

By now, long after all four original members have departed, a Ramones song, video, concert footage, or stray lyric floating around in my brain will connect me instantly to millions of people around the world. A generation later, the light and joy in the eyes of my students when they see a Ramones poster on my office wall says it all.

My name is Donna and I'm a sociologist. The Ramones have been a de facto higher power for over forty years. Even now, post-ascension, they're still my psychic protectors. Their music buffers me, as a participant-observer, against a social world I study formally but never fully engage with.

By day, as a graduate student in the early 1980s, I delved into the great works of Durkheim, Marx and Weber, Margaret Mead and C. W. Mills. By night, I embraced the sociology of the Ramones. So much of who I am has been informed by the Ramones' music. They offered a subterranean view of post–World War II America I could work with; high theory, low culture. So simple, so much fun, you might easily overlook how richly complex the music was, how sophisticated their lyrics were.

Before you realized it, you were abducted by the Ramones, sucked up into a cultural rebellion, a covert operation, a social movement. By the time you figured it out, the band had changed your life. Plus, the music was fun—fierce, energizing, loud, and fast. Vicious and wholesome and dark and hopeful, and all at the same time. Plus, they convinced us we could do it too; kids in the audience one night, onstage the next.

The Ramones penetrated the warped crevasses of the body social in sick new ways that resonated personally and culturally, prophesying in their specific time and place. Today generations of scholars, journalists, musicians, youth workers, filmmakers, artists, and clergy see the world through the punk prism most clearly articulated in the Ramones' project.

From the beginning, I was a fan, a true believer. Then, in 1996, as the Ramones were about to retire, my editor at the *Village Voice*, Ann Powers, asked if I wanted to interview them. After twenty-two years of service, now my boyz were saying *Adios, amigos*. Although they were my heroes, I'd never been interested in actually meeting them. I felt I already knew them, especially Joey. From their music, it was clear they knew me too. I rarely missed a show. The band lived inside my stereo speakers and my head. As my spiritual guides, the Ramones spoke to me in dreams. But I did need to get some quotes. It's widely known that the Ramones were one of rock's most dysfunctional families, complete with ongoing venomous intrigues and endless backstabbing. Johnny married Joey's fiancée; C.J. married Marky's niece, and it didn't end well. At any given time, Dee Dee hated

Joey or Marky. Or Joey was pissed off at Dee Dee. Or Johnny said something about Joey. The next week they were back, busy collaborating and setting up shows and deals. Together they were even more fucked up than my extended family. Alone, the Ramones could be the sweetest men in the world. Still, if you hung out with one, you didn't mention that you'd seen the others.

By 1996 I'd done my share of wacko interviews—Howard Stern, Mister Rogers, Eric Bogosian, Steve Malkmus. But interviewing the Ramones took all my social skills, and my life would never be the same. Tommy had retired ages ago, and at the time Marky was out of the country. Nobody could find Dee Dee. Everyone warned me Johnny told every reporter the same thing and that Joey would make me interview him twice. From what I gathered, C.J.—the bass player who replaced Dee Dee—was the only normal one. At the core of my teaching, my scholarship, and my spiritual journey is the study of human alienation. In the Ramones and their legions I found fellow travelers, a soul family of people who "get" me. By now, the Ramones' story has been told and retold in several forms and languages, across three generations. The names, dates, people, places, and things on their long tour of duty have been well documented. The Ramones of New York City were much greater than the sum of their documented achievements, awards, market shares, chart positions, and critical acclaim; they opened up the world for us. In recent years, we've enjoyed an outpouring of excellent Ramones biographies, memoirs, and oral histories, journalism, critical scholarly work, videos, bootlegs, documentaries, and feature films. C.J., Tommy, and the Ramones art director, Arturo Vega, too, have great stories yet to be told. But that's not my purpose here and now.

The work is part encomium, part eulogy, and I'm completely biased and prone to hyperbole. Like any diehard fan, I'm in an ongoing relationship with the Ramones' material, inclined to "creative readings" of their text, ever wondering, *What do they really mean?* I'm here to testify that the Ramones' music matters—culturally, historically, sociologically, creatively, and profoundly. In the early days of punk, as critics and scholars began to hail punks as the New Agents of History, the next Marxian messiahs, I began to understand the Ramones as the True Sons of the early-twentieth-century Italian neo-Marxist philosopher Antonio Gramsci. I embraced them as uniquely American organic intellectuals. They were of us, for us, and will remain with us, always.

Who were the Ramones? How have their individual and collective biographies intersected with us, with history? What did they stand for? What great gifts have they left for us? It's with great affection, reverence, joy, and sadness that I seek to add anything more to their story.

WHY
THE RAMONES
MATTER

1

The Mission

....

When he heard a Ramones cassette demo for the first time, the famously icy Lou Reed, in a rare moment of exuberance, immediately saw a crack in the order of things. "Without a doubt the most fantastic thing you've ever played me bar none. I mean, it makes everybody look so . . . wimpy, Patti Smith and me included . . . everybody else looks like they're really old-fashioned," Reed told Ramones manager Danny Fields. "That's rock 'n' roll. They really hit where it hurts." It was 1975, and rock and roll, as we knew it, was about to die. "They are everything everybody worried about—every parent would freeze in their tracks if they heard this stuff."

God gave rock and roll to you, and when it was lost in the wilderness, the Ramones were sent to earth to reclaim it. In order to be successful, rock and roll must scare the shit out of adults, cleanse the psyche of everyday bullshit, and energize the spirit. *Of the people, by the people, and for the people*, music heals, invigorates, educates, empowers, and uplifts, but above all, rock and roll is *fun*.

In the dark ages that preceded the Ramones, fans were shut out, reduced to the role of passive spectator. In the early 1970s, boredom had inherited the earth. The airwaves ruled by crotchety old dinosaurs, rock and roll had become *rock*. Formulaic and prefab, it was music as *rock product*, severed from its vibrant roots. Self-indulgent, bombastic, and overproduced: gone were the sounds of youthful angst, exuberance, raw power, rebellion, sexuality, and misrule. The very spirit of rock and roll had been beaten into submission, the glorious legacy bequeathed by doo-wop, Elvis, the Girl Groups, Chuck Berry, the British Invasion, and surf music, lost. Led Zeppelin, the Who, Black Sabbath, and AC/DC were still looming large, but they spoke to a different time and place. Increasingly, the commercially successful bands were Boston, Foreigner, Journey, Kansas. And then there was *disco*, punk's mortal enemy.

Rock-and-roll radio was nowhere to be found. So if you were an average American rocker kid approaching the mid-'70s, hanging out in your room, playing guitar, dreaming of being a musician, how could you possibly compete with maestros, inaccessible peacocks decked out in pricey vines, sporting expensive production and top-shelf equipment at million-dollar arena rock shows? You had no role models. You had Donny and Marie.

Playing live music was increasingly out of reach. Kids were disgusted; critics like Lester Bangs lamented the massive sell-out of stadium rock, the fancy guitar triplets and masturbatory ten-minute drum solos, an increasingly formula-driven music industry—going so far as to describe greedy record labels as "lecherous." And then suddenly, in 1974, a uniformed militia burst forth from Forest Hills, Queens.

Well, *stumbled* is more like it—the Ramones weren't all that uniformed at first; their early shows were more demented performance art than musical concert, with band members starting and stopping in fits, stage tantrums, infighting, cursing, and carrying on. It took the Ramones a while to cultivate their gifts. By the time they released their first album in 1976, they were a tight, efficient, smooth killing-machine that kept rolling hard for twenty-two years, nonstop, through dead-end suburbs, small cities, and towns and the stadiums of Europe, Asia, and South America, bringing kids the Good News about rock and roll.

In his autobiography, *Commando*, guitarist Johnny Ramone nails the band's Mission to the wall: the Ramones wanted to save rock and roll. The great bands of the past had been their idols. The Ramones were against what rock and roll was becoming — *no* rock and roll. "That's what we were against!" he writes. The result was a unique new sound rooted in teen music's forgotten past, replete with fresh styles, images, sounds, concepts, and strategies.

In the early 1970s a punk sensibility was already embedded in New York's underground music scene. In their pre-Ramones years, Tommy and Johnny were scene regulars catching NYC shows and making observations. The first time Johnny saw the New York Dolls perform he declared, "Hey, I can do that!" Tommy, too, was impressed with the trashy, glammy, gender-fucked band, and it hit him immediately; he thought about a few neighborhood guys he knew who could pull off a rock-and-roll band. The Dolls could barely play their instruments, but they were far more entertaining than most of the bands who could. For over a year, Tommy had been urging his friends to start a band — and here we are.

In 2005 Tommy told *Pitchfork*'s James Gregory, "The idea was just to get a charismatic, sort of quirky band together. But then when we got together, they were coming up with really great songs, which I hadn't even thought about. Once I saw that, I said, 'Wow, they could be more, they could be a real band.'" He credits Johnny with the Ramones' signature speed. Johnny was a baseball pitcher who loved throwing a fastball, he says. Plus, the guitarist was impatient, and that, with his love of velocity and the desire to demonstrate his virtuosity in a new form, set a new standard—the Ramones.

The New York Dolls, with their unpolished, raucous musicianship, exuberant style and flair, dressing up, and prizing entertainment and showmanship over mastery, had escaped the teenage wastelands of Staten Island and Brooklyn, landing in the creative center of the universe—Downtown. In a 2007 interview with the BBC, Tommy cited the Ramones' influences as the Dolls, Lou Reed, and Andy Warhol. This was a New York thing, and at first the punk scene, too, was an arty bohemia, avant-garde trash and vaudeville. According to Tommy, the early scene that developed at CBGB wasn't teen or garage based. It had an intellectual element the Ramones were part of. In a 1976 interview with *Rolling Stone*, Tommy explained the Ramones as the answer to the early 1970s, "when artsy people with big egos would do vocal harmonies and play long guitar solos and get called geniuses."

Early punk bands, including the Ramones, who considered themselves a *rock-and-roll band*, openly rejected the punk label out of hand. Still, the label helped critics identify a new genre, distinguishing it from the past, drawing attention to the scene. This allowed a new movement to surface and boosted the market—it sold records. The cultural youth rebellion we now call punk was the result of a cumulative, spontaneous, simultaneous, collective effort. Midwestern bands like Electric Eels, Rockets from the Tomb, the MC5, Death, and the Stooges; the Saints in Australia; and the UK's Sex Pistols, the Clash, and the Damned all had their hands in the sauce. Each contributed to the development of the local scene, styles, ideologies, and sounds of punk. But nobody played a greater part in proclaiming, defining, or pushing punk forward than the Ramones.

According to the journalist Stephen Thomas Erlewine, *the Ramones were the first punk rock band*. The Stooges and the Dolls may have prefigured them, and the bands that immediately followed, such as the Sex Pistols, made the "latent violence" of the music more explicit, but, he argues, "the Ramones crystallized the musical ideals of the genre." First they stripped the music down to its bare basics—four chords, catchy melody, demented lyrics. Then the Ramones accelerated the tempo, creating a revolutionary sound rooted in pre-Beatles rock and roll and pop. The Ramones are now widely acknowledged to be the *ultimate punk band responsible for the rise and reign of the genre*.

In his *Music Library of America* review of the album *Ramones*, Rick Anderson echoes what is now commonly accepted as rock-and-roll canon: that the Ramones delivered the very first, best declaration of the American punk ethic in 1976 in their debut album. Released in the summer of 2001 as a tribute to Joey, following his untimely death, the Ramones' first four albums, *Ramones*, *Leave Home*, *Rocket to Russia*, and *Road to Ruin* were remastered and reissued by Rhino. Reflecting on the reissues, Anderson writes that the first album's "bare bones instrumentation, aggressively minimalist song structures and goofy anarchic themes set the agenda for years to come."

In a 2016 homage, "The Ramones' Debut Album Is Still the Best Punk Record of All Time," the *Observer*'s Tim Sommer claims that *Ramones* marked the beginning of a new movement of music and style, "the public ascension of important artists." As musical revolutionaries, writes Sommer, the Ramones offered up "the best representation of the revolution they proposed." Their fierce rejection of guitar solos made "a shocking statement," far beyond more overtly "revolutionary" bands like the Clash and Sex Pistols, who regularly employed guitar solos. For Sommer, April 23, 1976, "marks the release date of one of the most skillfully executed and conceptually original recorded works of all time." He identifies *Ramones* and the Beach Boys' *Pet Sounds* as two of the "indisputably flawless albums" to have achieved such "conceptual and artistic perfection." Sommer considers *Ramones* "a deeply artistic, intentional record" and honors the "deeply intentional attempt to change history with an idea, and make history by executing it masterfully." Ben Sisario, writing for the *New York Times*, now considers *Ramones* "a founding document of punk rock." The Constitution.

Toward the end of 1974 the Ramones produced a fifteen-song demo for well under one thousand dollars. Tommy told the author Everett True that he did a lot of preplanning for this, laying down the tracks then returning a week later to mix it. "It was a smooth process," he said. "It felt like we were making important music. We knew we didn't sound like anyone else. It was funny and smart and good. We listened to old Beatles records—and because they were mono and then stereo the vocals could go on one side and the guitars on another. So that's what we did."

In *England's Dreaming*, Jon Savage describes the Ramones'

Donna Gaines

creative process—learning how to play onstage, fighting, slowly refining all the time. He describes their sound as a formalist's delight: "The mix was simple but artful: a minimal drumbeat (both channels) provided a basic structure for clipped vocals (centre); a bass guitar carried both melody and minimal rhythmic variation (left), and the guitar the sound (right) was merely a distorted, rhythmic texture." The first album now sounds laughably simple. But at the time, says Savage, it was brutal and divisive. After *Ramones*, everything else sounded ridiculously slow. As a reductio ad absurdum of the story of pop music so far—Beatles, Girl Groups, Beach Boys, Stooges, Herman's Hermits—the music, says Savage, was "pulped down into short songs that reflected the fragmented attention time span of the first TV generation." He concludes, "There was no melody, only distortion and sheer, brutal speed."

The songs were short, forceful, fast, and to the point. In 1975, interviewed by *Soho Weekly*, Tommy explained, "The Ramones wrote short songs for people who didn't have a lot of time." In their memoirs, Dee Dee has said the band's early works reflected their level of playing ability, and that the band played loud music because they liked to. Johnny claimed the songs were short because the band was so new to songwriting they couldn't write anything too complicated; it was nothing intentional. The guitarist was also inspired by the short set the Beatles performed at Shea Stadium, where in a punk-as-fuck move Johnny pelted rocks at the Fab Four. By the time the Ramones cut their first album, they had already compiled enough material for two or three more.

Musicians now consider the Ramones' first album a de facto

instructional manual for teaching yourself how to play by just listening, then working it out for yourself. When people complain that the Ramones' music has stayed the same over time, critics have argued, they are overlooking two things. First, that what the band accomplished out of the gate was perfect. Second, that the Ramones' orthodoxy demanded obedience to their particular artistic vision of purity in rock and roll. They would never waver.

In January 1976, the Ramones released their debut single on Sire, "Blitzkrieg Bop" backed by "Havana Affair." In September, the Saints from Australia released "I'm Stranded," the first punk record release outside the US after the Ramones but before the Sex Pistols or the Clash. The Ramones' eponymous first album was released in April 1976. Their summer of '76 UK tour can be regarded as the evangelical mission where the Ramones enlightened the Brits. November 1976 saw the release of the Sex Pistols' single, "Anarchy in the UK," followed up by their glorious 1977 debut album, *Never Mind the Bollocks*, causing a ruckus that gave the fledgling genre much-needed exposure.

Revolutionary War, July 4, 1976, London. The Ramones' first UK tour is often acknowledged as the moment the Pistols, the Damned, and the Clash got religion. In *Punk Rock Blitzkrieg*, Marky refers to this as "schooling British punk wanna-bes on English soil." In *End of the Century*, a documentary film about the Ramones, Joe Strummer recalls crowds of three thousand filling the spaces, groupies lined up to fuck the Ramones' roadies and managers—the true mark of rock stardom. But more important, how the Ramones inspired everyone to start their own bands.

At the time, Johnny Ramone was thrilled to meet all the aspiring punk bands. "They were cool-looking kids, which was what we needed for the movement." Johnny understood that the Ramones were changing the music, were situated at the forefront of something new, but he also knew the band couldn't do it alone. He viewed the UK bands and their fans as allies, people who could help advance the cause. The Ramones needed this new British Invasion—they had modeled their movement to reclaim rock and roll on the Beatles. "We were the Beatles and anyone else was part of it." Allied forces were crucial to the success of the Mission. The Mission was the music.

Although the early Ramones had their stateside supporters, in the years before alternative and college radio, it was the UK press and audiences who welcomed and up-charted the Ramones quickly and vigorously, unlike America's earthworms like that writer for the *Drummer* who huffed, "The last time I was insulted by something as bad as the Ramones was when Mary Hartman shot her husband in the crotch with a bow and arrow," or the dismissive "*Ramones* sounds more like greatest hits than a debut album" from *Village Voice* writer Richard Mortifiglio. The UK fans also innovated a unique punk dance form, the pogo, and later the mosh pit. In a tribute reminiscent of the early morning "gift" of a dead mouse your adoring cat presents you with bedside, the UK fans showed their love by spitting at their bands. The Ramones really hated that, being afraid of getting electrocuted onstage, saturated in phlegm, beer, and saliva. If Joey's lips touched the live mic, it would be all over. Well into the 1990s, in a YouTube video, C.J. can be heard onstage screaming at "the asshole with the Mohawk," swearing he'd kick the shit out of the kid if he didn't stop spitting. "It's not 1977!!!"

As Jon Savage explains, Malcolm McLaren, the legendary,

louche, and scheming manager of the Sex Pistols, had a plan to reboot the failing New York Dolls by luring the guitarist Syl Sylvain to the UK to start a band. But this never happened. From that broken dream the Sex Pistols were formed, infusing punk with great style, visual and sonic anarchy, and hard-peddling shock value that sensationalized the genre but compromised the Ramones Mission. While this was exciting and directed much-needed attention to the new music scene, the Pistols' mayhem cost the Ramones much-needed exposure. By 1978, after the Sex Pistols' disastrous first, last, and only tour, mainstream America was done with punk. The Pistols' San Francisco show at Winterland was their last. After that, the band broke up, but it was too late to make it right. Public perception lumped the Ramones and Sex Pistols together, piled on the garbage dump of pop culture.

The mediators—TV producers, most radio show hosts, and promoters—now dismissed punk artists as addicts, thugs, and ruffians. After the Sex Pistols, punk was rejected as messy teen anarchy, menacing and destructive, as *not music*. It would be that much harder for the Ramones to complete their Mission. To the gatekeepers of mass culture the Ramones were just another band of tattered hooligans who couldn't play. Dirty, ugly people gobbing and pissing all over everything. Meantime, the fans were all revved up and ready to roll!

The Ramones would go on to save some kids' lives and change many more—especially aspiring musicians'. Johnny Angel Wendell is an actor, musician, *Los Angeles Weekly* columnist, and radio host. He saw the Ramones for the first time at "the Rat" (Boston's legendary Rathskeller) on December 29, 1976. In the following three days, he bought their first record and a black leather jacket. He says, "I realized after seeing them that so much of rock music—in fact 90 percent of it by the mid-'70s—was unnecessary baggage. Little Richard, Chuck Berry, Eddie Cochran, and Buddy Holly designed the proper model, and the Beatles, Stones, Who, Kinks, and Lovin' Spoonful added on just enough without ruining it. As did the Velvet Underground, MC5, Stooges, Mott the Hoople, and the Dolls—but all of that was gone by 1976. The Ramones brought it back to tempo and refined it perfectly." Though the Ramones had a profound influence on him, he believes "they saved rock and roll a lot more than they saved my life."

The New York drummer Robert Holm remembers the first time he heard the Ramones. "My cousin Ray played me the first Ramones album in his basement, I was thirteen and he was twenty-three. I very clearly remember him showing me the cover and placing the album on the turntable and asking me what I thought of it. I thought it was funny. But a few weeks later my mother bought it for me and I played it endlessly for my friend Joe. Like many thirteen-year-olds, we thought it was funny at first, but then really got into it and turned all our thirteen-year-old friends on to it. We were definitely oddballs for liking it at that age," he says.

"It changed my life because it was the first kind of music that took me away from top forty radio. Definitely made me an outcast just cause I wasn't into Styx or whatever. But I enjoyed being on the outside with my odd friends. And it has stuck with me till this day." What's Holm's favorite Ramones song? "53rd." Why? "Killer bridge sung by Dee Dee!"

The Ramones' raw style resurrected the unholy spirit of

rock and roll, renewing old-school aesthetics, paying tribute to Americana, including imagery imported from the 1950s greasers, post–World War II motorcycle gangs, doo-wop, Girl Groups, bubblegum, and garage bands. They took *Tiger Beat* boy names and a fraternalized surname—Dee Dee's invention based on an alias once used by Paul McCartney. Or as Tommy joked, maybe the band just liked the way "ramone" sounded.

Their target look was basic street punk: skinny bodies wrapped in skintight ripped jeans, skimpy T-shirts, black leather biker jackets, and U.S. Keds. From a practical standpoint, the main thing any kid needed to be instantly recognizable as a Ramones fan was the Harley jacket; everything else most kids already had. No need for radical body modifications, hair, or gear. Beyond the early arty CBGB's spawning grounds, most young Ramones fans had to look normal for everyday life at school or work.

As an American band from New York City, the Ramones sustained their Mission by holding fast to American optimism and pride, against chronic obstacles, discouragement, and disappointment. They wanted to seize the airwaves, to celebrate the glory of rock and roll while addressing the encroaching gloom of growing up in the 1970s, just as the cracks in the American Dream were becoming visible. As Leonard Cohen reminds us, the cracks are where the light comes in, and the Ramones were punk's bringers of light. So whatever happened next—new wave's more commercially successful, synthesizer-driven, radio-friendly sound, feral hardcore's brutality, thrash metal, grunge, alternative—the Ramones, by sheer force, speed, stamina, originality, determination, and intention, matter. They are the Alpha and Omega of punk rock.

Establishing the Ramones' primacy as the progenitors of punk, their legendary eponymous first album is hailed by critics as "the shot heard round the world." Two hundred years after the American Revolution, the Ramones *changed everything*, stripping off yellowing layers of shellac, restoring the supremacy of rock and roll for the kids, the street, and the grand DJs of yore. When and where the Ramones entered history, millions followed.

At twenty-nine minutes long, *Ramones* was created in seventeen days for $6,400 at a time when superstars were demanding upwards of half a million. The Ramones resuscitated rock and roll, then they democratized it. Anyone could do it; you didn't need to be gorgeous, score a fat recording contract, book a fancy studio, hire a publicist, buy expensive clothes, or have the skills of Hendrix or Eric Clapton. You just had to follow Joey's credo: "Do it from the heart and follow your instincts."

Blistering through shitty equipment in small, moldy, smoky, ugly spaces, the Ramones helped rejuvenate the Bowery, giving New York fans a new reason to live; a subculture that quickly went viral, locally and then globally. As the utmost expression of individuality and uniqueness, "authenticity" replaced virtuoso mastery as the central tenet of punk musicianship. By 1979, writing in *Musician Magazine*, Lester Bangs was already a convert. "I love rock 'n' roll in its basest, crudest, most paleolithically rudimentary form." Bangs loved punk rock, no apology. What mattered most, he said, was that ordinary people were finding a voice. "I don't give a good goddamn if somebody can barely play their instruments or even not at all, as long as they've got something to express and do it in a compelling way." The Ramones set a new standard for rising generations of musicians learning to balance cult credibility with mass appeal. Punk was (and remains) an organic populist movement. As such, some bands sucked, many were great, and most were short-lived. But after the Ramones, control over the means of rock production had been permanently destabilized—DIY (do it yourself). According to an interview I did with Joey, the chorus in "Blitzkrieg Bop," "Hey ho, let's go," was "the battle cry that sounded the revolution, a call to arms for punks to do their own thing." Inspired by the Ramones' idols, the Bay City Rollers, the DIY message spread outward from the bowels of New York City to the UK and California, across Asia, into Latin America and Europe, instigating ten thousand new bands along the way. Lean, mean, clean, the Ramones ushered in a glorious new age of cultural engagement for the masses—local to global.

Now, more than forty years after the first album, long after the Ramones broke up in 1996, from Old Hanoi to East Berlin, punk ethics, values, styles, sounds, and sensibilities continue to permeate mainstream culture and society, offering alternatives and options. New dress codes, art, attitudes, and gender relations followed—girls do it too! From CBGB to Sleater-Kinney to Rancid and Green Day, the Ramones, stripped down with a streetwise antilook, speed-pop raw aggression, and darkly funny lyrics, influenced punk subgenres from new wave to hardcore, speed metal, and thrash. Infusing the sounds of alternative, grunge, riot grrrl, foxcore, and queercore.

The origin story of the Ramones has been told and retold around the world. Early on, amid dog shit, stale beer, and piss, CBGB's owner, Hilly Kristal, built a stage in the back of his Bowery biker bar and called it street music. In time, rock-and-roll history would be rewritten, with critics reclassifying bands like T. Rex, the Velvets, and the Dolls as "prepunk."

As the scene evolved into a subculture, new forms emerged to express it. Based in New York City, graphic artist John Holmstrom and writer Legs McNeil—two alienated, gifted high school friends from Connecticut—began documenting the scene in *Punk Magazine*, now considered one of the founding artifacts of New York punk history. Combining "comic book aesthetics with music coverage, *Mad Magazine*, animated children's cartoons, and writing songs that were almost cartoon parodies," this alliance unleashed a new form of street reporting, street art, and street music. This is what a bunch of arty juvenile delinquents can do if left to their own devices—DIY.

Established music critics were split on the merits of the first album, *Ramones*. Writing for the *Village Voice*, Robert Christgau gave it an A, explaining, "For me, it blows everything else off the radio: it's clean the way the Dolls never were, sprightly the way the Velvets never were, and just plain listenable the way Black Sabbath never was."

In his assessment of the Ramones during the 1980s, Phil Dyess-Nugent of *Burning Ambulance* explains that while the band was critically beloved, it was often misunderstood even by the smartest rock writers, including "West Coast chauvinist Greil Marcus" who "denounced them from their first onstage belch to their dying day for the same reason many East Coast chauvinists claimed to revere them—he took them for postmodern ironists."

In his 1977 review of *Rocket to Russia*, Marcus says, "*Ramones* and *Leave Home* (wonderful title) struck me as cold and ugly; I found the apparent irony of songs like 'Beat on the Brat' very unconvincing—as in a lot of rock and roll, irony here seemed like a mask the singer put on to disguise the fact that he meant exactly what he said. I also found those records dully one-dimensional. It's one thing to have a concept—lumpen-rock for lumpenoids (or people who get a kick out of touching the lumpenoid in themselves)—but you've got to have more than a concept to back it up."

"This is art," said Tommy Ramone in the liner notes for *Hey! Ho! Let's Go*. "Sometimes it doesn't sell at first. Sometimes it takes a while for the world to catch on." Over forty years later, I asked Marcus how he felt about the Ramones now. With the exception of "Bonzo Goes to Bitburg," one of the band's few overtly "political" songs, Marcus replied that the Ramones never meant that much to him, holding fast to his initial reaction. In contrast, the Portland-based critic Douglas Wolk captured the essence of the band's greatness (and essential goodness) when he asserted that unlike many of his imitators, "Joey Ramone never, ever sneered." The Ramones were in it for real. "There was a tenderness at the heart of their noisy attack that came from the band members' sincere commitment to what they were doing and to whatever audience wanted to hear them do it."

For a while, says Wolk, the greatest creative tension in the band was the split between Joey, who wanted to expand their territory to reach as many listeners as possible, and Johnny's fear that flirting with more commercial appeal would betray the audience who loved and needed the Ramones as they were. But Wolk concludes that neither choice—to chase a larger audience or serve a more exclusive one—was ever made cynically. "Both were, in their different ways, an expression of generosity."

To skeptics who complained that the songs all sounded the same, in 1975 Tommy dismissively told a New York City underground press's *Soho Weekly*. "Well, they didn't listen close enough." Give a listen to "Havana Affair" on the B-side of "Blitzkrieg Bop," their first single. And then check out "Pinhead" off *Leave Home*. The break is essentially the same few chords. "Loudmouth" and "I Don't Wanna Go Down to the Basement" are also very similar. The repetitive nature of Ramones music is not considered redundant by their fans. In fact, it may be the whole point. Oddly calming, like an amphetamine run; compulsive, offering soothing consistency: to the initiated no two Ramones songs will ever sound the same, each one inviting the listener to an entirely new adventure. The Ramones milked their three or four best riffs and then played them over and over again. Like Mosaic Law, once the sound was codified it stayed the same because it worked every time.

....

In the beginning, Douglas Colvin (Dee Dee) was the original Ramones vocalist, but the frisky bassist couldn't manage to sing and play at the same time, so over guitarist John Cummings's (Johnny's) objections, Jeff Hyman (Joey) took over as singer, leaving the band without a drummer. Tamás Erdélyi was the Ramones' manager and this swap of personnel was his idea. After a series of auditions he still had no luck finding a replacement, so Tamás became Tommy Ramone, their new drummer. Remaining on bass, Dee Dee would still call up each new song with his signature 1–2–3–4! count. Tommy began coproducing; drumming through the Ramones' first three albums, he famously practiced using a classical metronome with a flashing light to keep perfect time. As producer Craig Leon told the *New York Times*, "He looked like a little robot, like a member of Kraftwerk or something. He played straight to a metronome." Described by his admirers as a human metronome, Tommy kept the beat and served as the band's spokesman and distributor of flyers. After the third album he burned out, and in 1978 he left the band to produce them full-time.

Tommy was replaced by Marc Bell, formerly of the Voidoids; considered one of New York City's finest drummers, he was a Brooklyn boy, a lifelong musician and gearhead who favored vintage American cars, clothes, and who married his childhood sweetheart. As Marky Ramone, he built on Tommy's sound, pushing it further and harder. In his autobiography Marky describes tuning the snare higher and using larger cymbals, thus giving the sound "a bolder, more muscular feel."

Dee Dee had known Joey as Jeff Starship, a singer in a glitter band called Sniper who performed at the famed Queens club Coventry. Joey wore huge platforms and glitter garb, making him seven feet tall, quite the spectacle hitchhiking around Queens to the gigs. He was outrageous. Joey and Dee Dee were younger, in their early twenties. Like Tommy, Johnny was older, around twenty-five or so. He was already working full-time, with enough disposable income to rent an apartment, have his clothes made to order. Johnny subsidized his rock-and-roll dreams with a lucrative construction job he got through his father. He got married young to a local girl, half Jewish, half Egyptian, under a chuppah. Johnny had a sharp eye for hot cars, styles, and imagery and an ear for sound that influenced the direction the band would take. In time, he demonstrated a shrewd business sense as well.

Joey had a playful, open, curious spirit. He enjoyed recording the sounds of thunder, or basketballs bouncing off concrete, and was a walking encyclopedia of popular culture. At one point, Johnny had hair down to his waist and wore a headband. A few years older than Joey and Dee Dee, Johnny, like many former Queens hitters, briefly transitioned into a hippie by the grace of drugs and music, then gravitated to glam and glitter, and finally to the classic Ramones look he proudly wore for most of his life onstage and off. Johnny Ramone hated hippies. Dee Dee hated everyone.

Like most of New York's underground, the Ramones' early look had one foot stuck in glitter, because in 1974 the Dolls were still the shit. Everyone wanted to sound like the singer David Johansen—everyone except Joey. Glam offered kids an opportunity to dress up and make a scene with a subversive cultural agenda. As the British music writer Simon Reynolds shows in his 2016 book *Shock and Awe*, glam emerged in part as a first response to and rejection of all things hippie—the late '60s long hair, denim, no makeup for women, the intentional embrace of downward mobility. The hippies embraced a strict antigrooming policy, a norm of natural "earthiness" viewed as dull, boring, and above all, phony. In *End of the Century*, Legs McNeil describes the hippie era as mediocre and tedious, muted, brown. As a guy, you couldn't get laid, he says, unless you were "spiritual" or gave the chicks some rap about macramé. Tired of that scene, sick of that music, glam and its velvet jackets replaced washed-out denim; giant platforms replaced Birkenstocks; hair got styled up; the kids sparkled.

The Ramones' roots in early 1970s glam dovetailed with the rising gay rights and women's movements. As an assault on traditional gender roles and static sexual identities, and for the sheer fun of drag, glam continues to infuse music styles and sensibilities. Surfing the cultural trends from greaser to hippie, from glam to punk, each successive musical generation seeks to reclaim, renew, or reject the old forms in a spirit of *take what you need and leave the rest*. That's the engine of popular culture in history.

So tall, thin, shy, and gawky, Joey seemed a most unlikely rock star, sleeping on the floor of his mother's art gallery in Forest Hills, selling acrylic-dipped flowers in Greenwich Village, creating art by painting with vegetables. Dee Dee soon moved into the gallery. Like Joey and Johnny, he was trouble (and troubled) at home, at school, and on the street. Typical neighborhood guys, Dee Dee lived next door to Johnny, who was in a band with Joey's brother, guitarist Mickey Leigh. Johnny had known Tommy since high school—they'd had a band called Tangerine Puppets. It was Tommy who pushed the others to take the band seriously, to become musicians.

Tommy had a vision. The architect of the Ramones, onstage he directed where each member stood, emphasizing that the singer must not move and that there should be no spotlight. Tour manager Monte Melnick and band manager Danny Fields, early witnesses, have testified that the band was Tommy's concept. According to C.J. Ramone, who replaced Dee Dee on bass in 1989,

Tommy was the mastermind behind the Ramones—the band was his creation, from the look to the sound, attitude, and intention.

After graduation Tommy got a job as a recording engineer, setting up Performance Studios, a rehearsal space on Manhattan's East Twentieth Street. It soon became a showcase for early Ramones shows; two-dollar cover, mostly friends. To that end, the band famously rode the NYC subway system to their early shows and rehearsals, carrying their instruments in shopping bags. Some mythologies portray the Ramones' music as accidental. Not so. Tommy was already a professional soundman who worked on Hendrix's *Band of Gypsys*. Self-taught, diligent, offbeat, with a workingman's ethic and a soldier's sense of loyalty, each member of the Ramones embraced persistence and duty. And, of course, they were fucked up.

Typical American kids—anomic, clueless, unformed, chemically dependent, barely straddling early adulthood—pre-Ramones, the guys gravitated to each other, as Dee Dee explains in *Lobotomy*: "People who join a band like the Ramones don't come from stable backgrounds, because it's not that civilized an art form. Punk rock comes from angry kids who feel like being creative." As angry kids, Dee Dee says, the Ramones were all "the obvious creeps in the neighborhood, no one would have ever pegged any of us as candidates for success in life." But the music called to each of them and pulled them into a new world. In retrospect, their tour manager, Monte A. Melnick, says it's remarkable that Dee Dee and Joey, two "total nut jobs who can't keep everyday life in order," could achieve what they did.

Like most restless kids stranded on the wrong side of the bridges and tunnels of New York City, the Ramones knew heaven was just a train ride away on the Bowery, at CBGB, a scene pioneered by out-of-state boarding-school buddies Richard Hell and Tom Verlaine of Television, Blondie, and the college-educated Talking Heads—Johnny dismissed them as "a bunch of intellectuals." Meantime, up the road a piece at Max's Kansas City, bands like the Heartbreakers, Senders, Wayne/Jayne County, and Cherry Vanilla reigned supreme, but the Ramones were CB's boys (nobody ever called it "CBGB").

Shredded, psychotic, disorganized, and unruly onstage, at first the Ramones had people wondering if they could play at all. But that wasn't the point; their twenty-minute sets of rapid-fire, under-two-and-a-half-minute songs earned them a recording contract before any of their contemporaries, except for the shaman poet Patti Smith. You had to be sophisticated to realize the Ramones weren't d-u-m-b. But if you took them too seriously, you'd miss the point.

The way Joey clipped his words made people wonder if he was serious, sarcastic, spoofing, goofing on you, or all of the above. He deployed an eccentric phrasing that was a mixture of regional dialect and Britboy bastard inflection. There was something deranged and completely unique about a guy from Queens singing in a bad British accent. At 6'5", bone skinny, with bad posture, massive hair, and purple-tinted shades covering his face, Joey Ramone made a striking lead singer. Floating around somewhere within a tenor range with hints of baritone, Joey's quirky voice was distinctive and recognizable, the voice of American punk. Where many punks screamed their lyrics, Joey actually sang. Ironically, his singing style seemed to get worse the more he tried to make it legitimately "good."

Over the years, Joey's voice deepened as the music evolved and the band experimented with new producers, never wavering far from the original formula. Joey's voice was especially versatile during live shows when the music was faster, the nuances shifting as inflections and phrasing worked to accommodate the accelerated speed of an already manic pace. So we hear Joey dropping off whole syllables on songs like "I Don't Want to Go Down to the Basement"—*I don't wanna go down to the baaaee*—like he's too cool to bother finishing his words. But hey, daddy-o, it was a practical solution.

A viewing of recorded live shows over time demonstrates ever-changing linguistic and vocal inflection. Joey never sounded bored or scripted, and maybe that's why. He kept fucking around with the words like a kid playing with old toys, finding new ways to stage and rearrange them. Like Johnny's guitar playing, Joey's singing evolved as a result of trying to be normal, failing miserably, finding his own voice as an unintended consequence, and then perfecting it through practice and hard work.

The Ramones' music was itself a miracle of originality and innovation—something we discover serendipitously when we can't do what we're told we should do; a metaphysical axiom. Still, the singing lessons Joey took in the early years paid off; his rich voice lasted well beyond the Ramones until his last days.

The Ramones innovated unique stage imagery: Dee Dee and Johnny never smiled; and for generations, punks refused to smile for the camera. They stood onstage in fierce stomp position like bad boys. Legend holds that when the Sex Pistols first met the Ramones, Johnny Rotten was scared of them, afraid they would kick his ass—they were from New York! He thought they were gang members. John Holmstrom recalls looking into their eyes, especially Dee Dee's and Johnny's, knowing they could beat the shit out of you. Ramones were intimidating, stoic, aggro, legs spread apart; staring psychotically at their instruments, doing high splits, jumps, with instruments hung low. Joey's long, lean body was firmly planted and in your face, leaning in toward the audience, surgically attached to the microphone stand, glued to the floor yet coming at you, front and center. Teenage music was back; it was terrifying, exhilarating.

Sometimes Johnny's white Mosrite guitar turned totally red; with his hyperfast eighth-note down-picking revving up at an estimated speed approaching 200 bpm or higher, hands close to the strings, heavy on the wrist action, Johnny played with such ferocious fury his fingers bled. Johnny's "guitar solo" on "I Wanna Be Sedated" astonished critics; he played it on one single note. While Joey and Marky liked hard rock, including metal's festive power chords in a broad blues field, Johnny hated the blues as well as jazz, defining the Mission in musical terms: "We're playing rock & roll with no blues or folk, or any of that stuff."

As Legs McNeil tells Jon Savage, punk's rejection of blues was anti-hippie, not anti-black. "We were going 'Fuck the Blues,' 'Fuck the Black Experience.' We had nothing in common with black people at that time." McNeil explains that kids had endured ten years of being politically correct and now they wanted to have fun, since that's what kids are supposed to do. Defining a new genre means differentiating from, even rejecting the previous subculture. There must be a complete ideological break, a repudiation of the old ways. Any shred of hippie culture had to be expunged. The long guitar solos of classic rock were rooted in the blues. Led Zeppelin, the Stones, Clapton, and Elvis had "borrowed" heavily from black music. Punks viewed this appropriation as yet more proof of the hypocrisy that further alienated them from the hippies. In an early issue of *Punk Magazine*, McNeil explains, "We don't believe in love or any of that shit." Class antagonism was also at play, especially for the Ramones' legions. The social location of hippie subculture was the college campus. For punk, it was the street.

Early punk fans were boys, white boys. The kids of color and the girls came later, and when they did they brought it hard. In her 1977 reflection on punk, cultural critic Ellen Willis, noting the inherent misogyny in the punk stance, was wary of the new genre and its promise of revolt against musical and social pretension. Ramones music is presexual, like bubblegum pop, teeny-bopper, yet traditionally "masculinist," propelled by pure aggression and rage typically associated with male gender-culture and biology.

Though sentimental, there's nothing hot, lusty, or sensual about the Ramones' music. Their early material was full of militaristic references, Joey singing about the KKK, the CIA, and the FBI with the same forceful intensity that lacerated Johnny's hand. The now famous "Blitzkrieg Bop" was the Ramones' version of the Port Huron Statement of 1962—the political manifesto by the Students for a Democratic Society (SDS) that sparked the student activist movement. "Blitzkrieg Bop" was a new declaration of cultural refusal, social difference, and musical skill.

According to Ramones insider George Seminara, an award-winning filmmaker and photographer, Johnny micromanaged the staging with precision and perfection. Band members were strictly instructed to walk back to front, never across the stage. This was a practical consideration, to avoid tripping over the wires. Dee Dee and later C.J. were both wild men onstage, animated and flamboyant performers. But they were constrained by the lack of wireless technology. Besides, says Seminara, Joey enjoyed spinning his mic like Roger Daltrey, sometimes slamming his bandmates in the head. It had to be controlled.

Powerful, masterful, and intimidating onstage, by 1975 Dee Dee was a dedicated Fender Precision man, his weapon slung to the knees, bass lines soaring past at the speed of light, setting a new standard for generations of punk bassists to come. In 2014 Fender would name an instrument after him: the "Fender Dee Dee Ramone Precision Bass." The Ramones made everything look so simple. It wasn't. Like the Gospels, the Ramones delivered complex musical and literary truths with graceful simplicity—accessible and crafted for maximum audience engagement.

The Ramones' minimalist aesthetic was at the root of their Mission, best articulated in Dee Dee's Queens logic: "I think rock & roll should be three words and a chorus, and the three words should be good enough to say it all." *Rolling Stone*'s Mikal Gilmore credits Dee Dee as the "complex addled essential spirit and the center of the Ramones brilliant and damaged story. Without him, the band would not have made as much great music at any point in its life span."

Early on, Tommy's no-nonsense drumming set the tone. "He gave punk rock its pulse," read the *New York Times* obituary headline in 2014. With his furiously "metronomic eighth notes and tribal floor-tom bombs," Tommy provided the speed-freak beat on the Ramones' groundbreaking first three albums, matching tempos with Dee Dee's mania and Johnny's punishing buzz-saw guitar. "Not unlike a fast drill on a rear molar" was how Tommy characterized his own style. Aspiring and established drummers alike remain awed by Tommy's skill and stamina, playing eighth notes on a high hat at warp speed, each song a minute and a half, for up to two hours, nonstop—live. Tommy's drumming set the standard for the Ramones' perfect, tight, unified para-military assault. Influenced by Jan and Dean and the Bay City Rollers, Tommy told Timothy White of *Rolling Stone* how the deep, densely packed Ramones sound worked. "We used block chording, as a melodic device, and the harmony resulting from the distortion of the amps created counter melodies." The wall of sound, he explained, was used as a melodic rather than a riff form, creating what he described as "a song within a song cre-ated by a block of chords droning." Lovely candy-coated pop mel-odies delivered with an earsplitting guitar; upbeat, simple tunes with silly lyrics slamming social truth across the world. Rude, real, raw, and raging.

With a few dark tweaks from Dee Dee, Tommy wrote the Ra-mones' anthemic "Blitzkrieg Bop." Johnny also credits him with the band's look. Tommy realized it had to be uniform in order to gather in the exiles. "Middle America wasn't going to look good in glitter and we needed a more streamlined image," he writes. "Glitter works for perfect bodies, it wouldn't work for most Americans." The Ramones wanted something the everykid could relate to; simple, timeless. The uniform is easy to assem-ble: unisex, basic, artlessly cool today as it was then.

Expansion of the fan base—central to the Mission itself—meant maximum *inclusion*. This was the Ramones' Principle of Love, the opposite of urban, arty bohemia's condescension, critic snark, and the dominant order's institutionalized practice of indifference and cultural exclusion. The Ramones were nonaffluent, undereducated American kids who embraced traditional aspirations; they wanted to be rich and successful, rock stars—as big as the Beatles. Above all, Johnny wanted to make a living doing something more fun than construction, earning enough to retire and live a good life. The rock-and-roll version of the American Dream.

America formed the Ramones. In turn they upheld a lifelong belief in the emancipatory promise of rock-and-roll radio: the Top Forty seven-inch vinyl, three-minute hit single. They embraced popular culture, everything from McDonald's to baseball. This was American folk music for the children of consumer society's crowning achievement: mass culture. Joey wrote "Chain Saw" after seeing *Texas Chain Saw Massacre*, rhyming *massacreeeeee* with *me*. Johnny's "I Don't Wanna Go Down to the Basement" is an ode to all the B-movie horror flicks he loved. Likewise, "Pinhead" is a cooperative effort inspired by the 1932 horror film *Freaks*. "Havana Affair" is a fictional spy movie from kids who grew up on *I Spy* and the *Avengers*, Marvel Comics and Spiderman.

In his autobiography, *Punk Rock Blitzkrieg*, Marky offers a comprehensive accounting of boomer childhood artifacts that filled each Ramones imagination, and ours: the Slinky, Play-Doh, Mr. Potato Head, Lionel train sets, plastic models of cars, ships, and planes, Universal Studios monsters—the Mummy, Dracula, Wolf Man, the Creature from the Black Lagoon—all of it infused in the Ramones' creative process. The Three Stooges, *Mad Maga-*

zine, Abbott and Costello on TV, the *Adventures of Superman*. The atomic bomb, the Cuban Missile Crisis, Soviet spies, the "duck and cover" drill. Whatever the Ramones could surgically remove from the zeitgeist was captured, quickly warped, rendered sick as possible; twisting it, they devoured it then fed it all back to us on a vinyl platter.

....

E Pluribus Unum. Although they were often treated like pariahs in the land of their birth, the Ramones always called themselves an American band. Patriotic, goofy, innocent, and too tough to die, they were individualistic yet inclusive, eccentric yet populist; the Ramones stood firm, a uniformed, fighting army. "I saw them as the ultimate all-American band. To me, they reflected the American character in general—an almost childish innocent aggression," Ramones art director Arturo Vega tells Jim Bessman. On creating the band's iconic logo, Vega explains, "I thought the great seal of the president of the United States would be perfect for the Ramones, with the eagle holding arrows —to symbolize strength and the aggression that would be used against whoever dares to attack us—and an olive branch, offered to those who want to be friendly." Instead of the olive branch, says Vega, the design incorporated an apple tree branch, "since the Ramones were American as apple pie." And since Johnny was such a baseball fanatic, Vega had the eagle holding a baseball bat instead of arrows.

Although a high lottery number saved him from the draft, Commando Johnny was so American he hated to leave our shores. The former military school student still folded his clothes army style on tour but did his best to avoid jury duty and was grateful for a high draft lottery number. In his autobiography he cites "gaming the system" as his highest goal. A self-described conservative who blamed affirmative action for the loss of his construction job, Johnny Ramone's brand of politics and his irrepressible urge to fuck with people added an edge to the music; it likely broadened the band's appeal as well.

Johnny was a little xenophobic. A homebody, he describes sitting in the car on tour in the UK while the other Ramones visited Stonehenge to "look at a pile of rocks." He was so disgusted he wouldn't let his girlfriend, Roxy, leave the car either. "Filthy and disgusting," he complains of UK hospitality, the dirty toilets, lack of electricity, and bad food—"curry shit." France, says Johnny, made him downright "suicidal." He refused to sleep there ever again, demanding to be taken out of the country after every gig. Johnny never forgave the Republic for its bad behavior in World War II or its ongoing anti-Americanism. Although he loved touring in Spain and Sweden, being overseas wore him out. "I'm so Americanized that anything else was hard for me to deal with." No ice, warm Coke; no special-order options for fast food; if you hated pickles, you had to scrape them off. And "you sure weren't going to get someone who spoke English at Burger King." Punk patriotism meant eating fast food too!

Even in America, after a show Johnny preferred to stay in his room, watching TV, unwinding with milk and cookies from 7-Eleven. The Ramones' lives, their collective quirky, antisocial eccentricities, their contradictory personalities, and all their obsessions *was* their music. They were completely themselves at all times—the good, the bad, and the ugly. The 1980s were especially challenging, with growing interpersonal toxicity at an all-time high, but stamina and persistence paid off. The Ramones became one of the most prolific, hard-touring bands ever, outlasting the other contenders. As Johnny explains, "Music we made by the seat of our pants against all odds became timeless."

Actually, they didn't have a choice; for too many years touring was the only way the Ramones could make a living. Trapped in the Ramones' fifteen-seat Econoline tour van for over twenty years, relegated to assigned seats, courtesy of El Jefe Johnny, this was not a happy family, but a family nevertheless. Infamous for their venomous band relationships, the Ramones nevertheless sustained an all-for-one, one-for-all work ethic with regard to the music. This prevailed even as personal relationships, setbacks, and disappointments hardened them. Placing unity over self-interest for the good of the band, the Ramones rose to the occasion. Whether hungover, dope sick, or going mental, even with Joey's best-kept secret—the lymphoma he chose not to disclose to unsympathetic bandmates for several years—the Ramones were disciplined.

From all accounts, Johnny's leadership bordered on authoritarian; though charismatic, talented, funny, shrewd, and determined, he could be domineering, dictatorial, and often abusive —verbally and sometimes physically. The Ramones Rules set forth in "Commando" were nothing compared to Johnny's touring regulations: No food. In addition to his chronically dirty socks and the stench of Joey's chronically infected feet, Johnny feared that food would further stink up the van. Tommy has described Johnny as a contradiction, a mystery, with different personalities. Ramones tour manager Monte Melnick describes Johnny as Mr. Negativity, a "very controlling person who radiated anxiety and fear." Tommy recalls seeing kindness and compassion in Joey's eyes, and only coldness in Johnny's. In his autobiography, Johnny reflected on how he felt himself. "I can't be weak, ever, because I'm locked into this, and this is how people see me."

The band ate their meals at Cracker Barrels across the land. Restaurant policy stated that for a signed photo the whole entourage ate free. Marky's sense of humor and his Brooklyn-bred cojones kept him out of Johnny's firing range. Marc Bell has denied reports that he habitually snatched leftover food off strangers' plates but does confirm he ate bugs—including windshield roadkill—on a dare and a bet. Once before a show, Johnny curtailed this activity. He was pragmatic; he didn't want Marky getting sick before the Ramones had to play.

It was now Johnny's band, Johnny's rules. Dee Dee noted that even though Johnny barely wrote a song, he still considered himself the boss and reigning authority on all things musical. Fixated at whatever age they had started getting high, working as full-time musicians since early adulthood, the Ramones combated road fatigue with *Lord of the Flies* pranks, bullying, scapegoating, and sometimes beatings by Johnny. No smoking cigarettes. Pot was okay because it sedated a manic Dee Dee, but no drinking in the van.

Uniquely for rock-and-roll bands, Ramones wives and girlfriends were welcomed on tour. It had a stabilizing effect on the band. Besides, as Johnny explains, the early Ramones' fans were mostly boys. "We never had that many hot women hanging around our shows except in California and Texas. Mostly, punks are misfits and those certainly aren't the kind of girls you want." This noxious statement may reflect band members' psychotic early romantic relationships, mutually abusive and violent (for example, Dee Dee and Connie, Johnny and Roxy). They were in their early twenties at the time, when "love" is more like psychosis.

With Dee Dee's ongoing mental health issues and cross-addiction, Joey's obsessive-compulsive disorder, and a growing alcoholism they both shared with Marky, control freak Johnny's nerves were shot. With no clinical understanding of OCD or bipolarity, sequestered on the endless road with no treatment plan on the horizon, Johnny did what he had to do. An ex-junkie who had a life-altering spiritual awakening at age twenty, Johnny viewed Joey's behavioral quirks as irresponsible, unorganized, and chaotic. He was intent on getting things done no matter what. Nothing was to stand in the way of the Mission. Fear of economic insecurity haunted Johnny. Notoriously frugal, on the road he ate canned sardines, even on tour in France, where he hated the food anyway. Even on his wedding day to Linda, Johnny admits he scrimped on his bride's rented plastic flowers.

The notoriously smelly Econoline van has been described as a rock-and-roll day hospital on wheels, with Johnny's endless racist tirades and anti-Semitic taunting of Monte, Tommy, and Joey, and his bullying and belittling of an immobilized Dee Dee. Johnny was known as a tough guy in middle-class Forest Hills, but as he himself notes, this wasn't like being tough in the Bronx or Brooklyn—it was pretty nice. "So I had the intimidation factor in this very Jewish Neighborhood. The other kids just weren't brought up to be tough." The tough Jews, like the Dictators, were in the Bronx.

With Tommy gone, as the self-appointed leader of the band Johnny sat shotgun in the van, commandeering the radio dial, tormenting his passengers with endless hours of Rush Limbaugh and baseball game broadcasts. Dismissive of Joey's OCD and the bizarre behaviors that often delayed and derailed road trips, Johnny explains: "It wasn't as if we were the models of sanity, so if someone is a nut, great, we *are* the Ramones after all. I just didn't want to know about it. I didn't care about it." The immaculate Dee Dee, who took several showers each day, was freaked out by Joey's gnarly hygiene. He also believed that everyone hated him, that nobody cared about him. Dee Dee as pincushion, a perpetual victim-boy.

If Johnny was Mean Daddy Ramone, charged (by default and by design) with the instrumental tasks of leadership, the Mommy job fell to Monte. As the band's patient and "long-suffering" roadie-turned-tour-manager, Monte was charged with coaxing Joey into the van following hours of the singer's OCD rituals, or combing the streets for an MIA Dee Dee who'd escape the van to go cop. Monte was Tommy's close friend from Forest Hills. They met in junior high school and were in several bands together, Monte on bass and Tommy on guitar, playing first in Triad, then later in Butch. Members of the Ramones have openly acknowledged that Monte was the more talented, accomplished musician among them, with several albums to his credit. He also needs to be canonized in some religion for dealing with their shit for so many years.

To date, Monte A. Melnick remains the dedicated keeper of the Ramones' flame, the last man standing, sharing a lifetime of sharply insightful Ramones memories in his acclaimed oral history, *On the Road with the Ramones*. He is an icon in his own right, with tribute bands dedicated to him—including the Melnicks, and Monte's Revenge—and he still lives in Queens. Monte and Arturo Vega are the fifth and sixth Ramones respectively. Vega, of Chihuahua, Mexico, was a roadie who became the Ramones' landlord and art director.

The Ramones have had five drummers: first Tommy, then Marky, then Richie Ramone, who stepped in after Marky's drinking took him down. Billy Rogers—who had played with the Heartbreakers, the Senders, and the Slugs—sat in for the recording of the Ramones' cover of "Time Has Come Today." Marky refused to play on the Chambers Brothers classic because he didn't think it was Ramones music. He was also bottoming out on alcoholism. Elvis Ramone, aka Clem Burke, Blondie's drummer, also joined the Ramones for a few weeks. Once Marky got sober, he reclaimed his position and went on to do great things. For anyone struggling with addiction, Marky's autobiography portrays the life of a true musician with an independent spirit who matures into a grateful sober man of dignity and grace.

In 1989 Dee Dee finally imploded from long-standing creative frustrations. Chronically overmedicated and sick of Johnny's overregulation, he quit cold turkey—got off all his meds, left his marriage, and quit the Ramones. He wanted to be a hip-hop star, renaming himself Dee Dee King after Stephen King, following the success of *Pet Sematary*. Hip-hop's call and response form should have worked well for a storyteller as gifted as Dee Dee, now replete with gold chains, chunky rings, new hair, and a whole new look. With support from the Ramones' first label, Sire, Dee Dee recorded *Standing in the Spotlight*, but it never hit.

He formed other bands and kept writing songs for the Ramones; he published an autobiography and a novel and had several art shows. Multitalented, Dee Dee's escape from the band renewed his creative spirit, but it failed to deliver the inner peace and commercial success he hoped for.

The Ramones needed a new bass player. AWOL from the United States Marines at the time, Christopher Joseph Ward of Long Island became C.J. Ramone, transfusing the band with much-needed youthful energy. C.J. played bass with edgy vitality and great humility. "I tried not to look like I'm taking someone else's place, but go up there to do my job and entertain people." After they arrested him and shaved his head, C.J. cleaned up his mess with the Marines and joined the band. The new bassist looked up to Johnny, whom he viewed as a second father. It was Johnny who insisted on hiring C.J. Marky was less convinced; Joey left the decision to Johnny. Born in Queens on October 8, the same day as Johnny, C.J. was a quick study, well disciplined, obedient to the Ramones' order, as Johnny knew an ex-Marine would be. He quickly mastered Dee Dee's signature jumps, mid-air splits, bouncing, grimacing, and signature call, 1–2–3–4!

Of his time in the military, C.J. told a reporter for punktastic.com: "Had I not spent time in the USMC I would have never lasted. I would have been kicked out of the Ramones pretty quickly because I had no self-discipline and I hated anyone telling me what to do. Johnny ran a tight ship and there were no grey areas. I fit right in." Regarding the Marines, he said, "Had I not served, I'd have drank and partied until I was dismissed or dead. I am who I am because of my time."

In retrospect, hiring C.J. was one of the best things the Ramones could have done. Viewed by some as a better musician than Dee Dee, he was liked by all the young girls. By now Nirvana was rising, Seattle was exploding, and the alternative scene was taking over. Grunge was about to permanently displace hair metal. C.J. emerged as the missing link between the two generations. Born in 1965, fourteen years younger than Joey, sixteen years younger than Johnny, C.J. is part of the baby bust generation's first battalion. He's credited with extending the life of the band, expanding the fan base to a new audience—Gen X kids. With the emergence of second-generation punk bands like Green Day and Rancid, the Ramones' legacy was further elevated.

The Ramones didn't see the new bands as competition but as loyal fans—even as their financial success far eclipsed that of the Ramones. The young punks honored their fathers with awe and reverence, and in turn were beloved by their exalted punk predecessors. The offspring achieved far more than the generation before them: they owned the airwaves; their albums ran gold and platinum; they sold out arenas; they were hailed as rock stars. Once upon a time, sacrificing so that your children would have more was part of the American Dream. But it's never too late to catch another wave. In the 1990s, thanks to the Gen X bands and their fans, the Ramones' phoenix began to rise up from the ashes. This invigorated their final years, further solidifying their place in rock-and-roll history.

C.J.'s song "I Got a Lot to Say" on *Adios Amigos*, their final album, offers a brilliant end-of-career statement for the band, showcasing C.J.'s talents as a songwriter. With only two lines and a few more chords than that, it's comical, provocative, economical, and incisive. In the first line, he has a lot to say; in the second, he can't remember. That's it! Written within the traditions established by Dee Dee, the song perfectly summarizes the Ramones' unique songwriting genius. The song could have easily been placed on their first album twenty years earlier. It stands today as a corollary to *Ramones'* "I Don't Wanna Walk around with You," and it's perfect.

Friendly and outgoing, with roots in metal and cute sisters all the young Gen X bands liked, C.J. befriended Soundgarden, Pearl Jam, and others, introducing them to the more insular, standoffish Johnny, whom they rightly viewed as a rock-and-roll legend. This exposed the guitarist to a new world of musicians and friends from the West Coast.

After the Ramones retired in 1996, Johnny never played again, convinced that nothing would ever be as good as being a Ramone. Johnny ultimately retired to LA, where he lived out the rest of his life with Linda at their "Ramones Ranch." He continued to harbor secret fantasies of a Ramones reunion. But once Joey had passed, Johnny knew it was over forever. Though they may have hated each other as people, like any fucked-up family they remained bound together in this life as brother Ramones, ultimately placing Mission principles over personalities.

Tommy created the Ramones, but Johnny, for all his creepy shit, was the truest believer in the Mission. I first met him in 1996 at the Empire Diner in Chelsea. The Ramones were retiring; Johnny was moving to Los Angeles—*Adios, amigos.* "Here I am talking to you, a left-wing paper," he said. "I want our fans to know that I don't read it." When his friends found out he was being interviewed by the *Voice,* they made fun of him: "You're gonna talk to that Commie paper?" Johnny defiantly pointed to his T-shirt: "Kill a Commie for Mommy."

Interviewing Dee Dee or Joey could last all day, and the topics covered everything under creation. Johnny met with me at a public place; Dee Dee and Joey, in their homes. Johnny was punctual, no drama or mood swings. Professional. In long hours, Dee Dee and Joey gave you everything—blood, tears, pizza, truth, and love. They lived in the moment. In contrast, Johnny's answers seemed scripted, served up as a paper plate of canned vegetables; stale catechism. The street on Johnny had always been that he was a heartless prick. Dee Dee and Joey had no boundaries; Johnny had too many.

Three Ramones in three years. People called it the "Curse of the Ramones." Soon after, their friends and associates began dropping off, dying one right after the other. In *Poisoned Heart*, Dee Dee's first wife, Vera Ramone King, relates the unsettling tale of a dark stormy night in Tulsa, Oklahoma, in 1978. Following a show, the Ramones' entourage encountered a zealous preacher dressed in a long black leather coat. He began ranting and raving, warning the group of deadly doom and hellacious gloom if the Ramones did not repent of their evil ways. Afterward, riding in the van, the group remained pensive and quiet. Vera wonders if that preacher put a curse on the band. People still suspect something.

April 15, 2001. At age forty-nine, five months before the twin towers went down, Joey Ramone passed away following a lengthy battle with lymphoma. Joey's positive worldview is evident in his posthumous solo album, *Don't Worry about Me*, in the upbeat momentum of songs like "What a Wonderful World" and

"I Got Knocked Down (but I'll Get Up)." Today the shy loner, the former high school reject, is a personal hero. By just being himself, the "King of Punk" gave teenage outcasts everywhere something to believe in, an alternative to killing themselves or blowing up the high school.

Joey, Dee Dee, Johnny, Tommy, and Marky were formally inducted into the Rock and Roll Hall of Fame in March 2002 at the Waldorf Astoria by Eddie Vedder of Pearl Jam. I was there because I wrote their induction essay. That night Phil Spector hosted a party; Green Day and Rancid came to pay homage to the band that had made them possible. Dee Dee wore a wine-colored sharkskin tuxedo. Onstage at the podium accepting his award, he said, "Hi, I'm Dee Dee Ramone and, uh, I'd like to congratulate myself and thank myself and give myself a big pat on the back." Fans (and some Ramones principals) believed this was fitting since he had written most of the songs.

June 7, 2002. Dee Dee Ramone is found dead in his Los Angeles apartment of a heroin overdose by his second wife, Barbara Zampini, who had returned from work. I figured he was probably just fooling around, like a mischievous little kid playing with matches while the adults were away. He hadn't been using, but his system was too clean and the dope was too strong; it took him out like Sid Vicious. Dee Dee was the centrifugal force of the band's creativity: some people talked to rainbows; Dee Dee talked to Jesus. While the personal intensity of each Ramone exploded into a glorious whole far greater than the sum of its parts, Dee Dee is acknowledged as a true genius, with demonic wit and fierce longing for something he never found.

Vera Ramone King's memoir reads like a survival kit from a

devoted, kindhearted woman who emerges whole after years of denial and codependency, freed at last from life with an "addict's addict." More dangerous clean and sober than when using, long after he quit the Ramones, Dee Dee dreamed of murdering Joey and Johnny. On a good day Dee Dee was generous, brilliantly funny, and sweet. Occasionally he spoke in tongues, beat Vera mercilessly, and he compulsively collected tattoos, watches, rings, Nazi memorabilia, and switchblades. The Ramones' music is positive, energizing, and fun, but as Joey has noted, there's a dark side to it too, discernible in the music and the lyrics, rife with resentment, refusal, rage, and repulsion. For the fans this would prove to be crucial.

September 15, 2004. To this day some fans still dislike Johnny Ramone, dismissing him as an asshole, a bully, a "wife beater" (ex-girlfriend Roxy), a Republican, even a fascist. It is true that John Cummings went to military school, became a construction worker, and in his younger years was, by his own account, a petty criminal, a nasty Queens hitter. "I was bad every minute of the day," he said. He also loved clothes, America, and rock and roll. Teenaged Johnny was a street punk who enjoyed beating on people, breaking and entering, and dropping TV sets on the passers-by from the rooftops of Forest Hills apartment buildings with his pals for kicks. He was an angry guy. But in a moment of clarity he realized that wasting his life on stupid shit wasn't God's plan. When his band was inducted into the Rock and Roll Hall of Fame, Johnny Ramone, accepting his award, publically asked God to bless America and President Bush.

If Joey was the heart, Dee Dee the soul, and Tommy the visionary of the Ramones, Johnny was the balls, the propellant for punk's most dysfunctional family, drilling them through twenty-two years of hard touring, cross-addictions, personality crises, and bad breaks. In *End of the Century*, the Ramones' guitarist comes off as a merciless taskmaster who browbeat his bandmates into a tight paramilitary organization. He notoriously stole Joey's girl, Linda, then married her, breaking his bandmate's heart. The band kept touring, but Johnny kept Linda out of sight for fear Joey would quit. After that, Joey and Johnny never spoke again.

Although Marky and C.J. were in their prime as musicians, it was Johnny's decision for the Ramones to retire in 1996. He wanted the band to go out on top, not linger until they sucked. Toward the end of the *Adios Amigos* tour, an extraordinary lucrative offer appeared, a series of shows in Argentina with big money, massive audiences, and media exposure. Johnny wanted it bad, but Joey refused. He was too weak and sick. He pulled the plug.

In sadomasochistic relationships, the question always emerges, *Who did it to whom?* Who has the ultimate power, the control, the S or the M? Joey and Johnny had been at it for years, but Joey was no victim; he was stubborn, and he held grudges. He once told me, "I'll forgive, but I won't forget." Though Johnny mellowed with age, especially when he knew he was sick, he refused to call Joey, even as the lead singer lay dying in a hospital bed. But their relationship continued, even after Joey's death.

Throughout their career, the band was thwarted by what frustrated insiders have called "Ramones Luck," a toxic combination of bad timing, poor choices, and fate. For example, the band gets inducted into the Rock and Roll Hall of Fame, but Joey dies. Or

Donna Gaines

they would cheap out on a photo shoot or studio recording time. Pennywise, pound foolish; three steps forward, two steps back.

Seeing his own behavior toward his bandmates in the 2003 Ramones documentary, *End of the Century*, Johnny remarks, "It's accurate, it left me disturbed." Toward the end of his life, Johnny would acknowledge that Joey was *irreplaceable*. "Joey was our singer," he said, respectfully, with a trace of sadness, even affection. For Johnny, after Joey died, the Ramones were over forever. In some dysfunctional families, that's as good as love gets.

On Sunday, September 12, 2004, surviving Ramones and friends put on a tribute concert in LA for Johnny. He had been secretly sick for ten years with prostate cancer. Three days after the show, Johnny Ramone died, surrounded by his wife and closest friends—his work on earth was finished.

2

Ministry

....

Ask any fan, "Why do the Ramones matter?" *The Ramones Matter Because They Are the Fucking Ramones!! If I have to explain . . . duh!* Anyone reading a book about why the Ramones' music matters already knows the answer and would probably rather spit up than discuss it. Explaining why the Ramones matter is like . . . *surfing to geometry.* Yes, the Ramones hated everything, including geometry, the nine-to-five world, and the screaming spoiled brats of Forest Hills. But they loved chicken vindaloo, rock-and-roll radio, *surfinbrrrds*, horror movies, and TV. The Ramones loved New York City and America too. Most of all, they loved you.

The Ramones gave us many songs—songs of mirth and merriment, mayhem and madness, rage and resentment, sorrow and sadness. Their songwriting reflects a joyful obsession with popular culture and all things American: pizza, Carbona, Coney Island, Burger King, war movies, comic books, and soda machines. In their simple pop tunes we learn to laugh at ourselves and the world, celebrating what makes us unique, neutralizing the toxic residue of growing up *strange.*

If the Ramones Mission was to rescue rock and roll, they also had a Ministry: to draw the outsider in from the margins. By herding stray cats into a quirky soul tribe, the Ramones found their calling in the gathering-in of the outcasts. Steeped in humor and irony, rendered with kindness and respect, each one of the Ramones understood the alienation of the outcast. Catchy, clever, cool, the Ramones spoke truth to their fans in the language of the heart. *If the world hates you, know that it hated me before it hated you.*

As punk subculture was becoming more visible, Lester Bangs chillingly observed that many of the people around the CBGB and Max's scene seemed emotionally and physically crippled. He noted speech impediments, hunchbacks, limps, but most of all a spiritual flatness. "You take parental indifference, a crappy educational system, lots of drugs, media overload, a society with no values left except the hysterical emphasis on physical perfection, and you end up with these little nubbins." The kids were all fucked up and ready to go, but flaunting one's damage was a part of punk's appeal. Ramones fans were increasingly younger, scruffier, bridge-and-tunnel kids, more working class and suburban, especially in the years after the Ramones left home.

But the Ramones played for the kids, not the critics. Celebratory yet deadly serious, Ramones narratives walked us through the darkness, then made us want to start a band, chop our hair, shred our T-shirts, dance, and howl at the moon. Welcoming us into a better world—one they created just for us—they reaffirmed our dignity, offering courage and an arsenal of slogans to face the day. The Ramones encouraged us to see life as hilarious fun because they understood the terror of being all alone in the danger zone.

Dee Dee's "Lobotomy," a song written with the producer and guitarist Daniel Rey, expresses the personal agony of marginality, isolation, and loneliness. In lunatic rants like "Cretin Family," we get a back door into noxious family relations, a buffer zone, and a great laugh; in prayerful homilies like "I Believe in Miracles" (both written with Rey), a declaration of faith and hope. One Generation X couple I know incorporated the lyrics to "I Believe in Miracles" into their wedding vows, explaining, "Rock and roll is our religion"—pledging their faith in music and in a better world for all of us.

A few years after the band retired, long after Dee Dee had quit the Ramones, I ran into him on the Lower East Side. That day Dee Dee seemed especially out of sorts, upset. "I don't fit in anywhere," he said, explaining how he felt like a misfit. I was stunned. Dee Dee had lived all over Europe; North and South America too. He'd remarried, moved to the country, enjoyed tending to beloved pets; and he continued to write great songs and play music. Dee Dee's post-Ramones tribute project, the Remainz, featured wife Barbara on bass and vocals, Marky, and C.J. Sometimes Joey sat in as well. Dee Dee had toured the world, a place where everyone knew his name. He'd been a hip-hop artist, a painter, a writer, featured in films and on TV; and of course, he was a Ramone. And still he wondered, *Where do I belong?* Astonished that one so beloved would feel so alone, I said, "Dee Dee, you don't *have* to fit in. We all fit in with *you!*"

Weren't millions of fans and friends and a loving wife proof enough that he was wrong? The Post-Ramones Empire now included generations of fans crossing boundaries of race, religion, sex, nation, and age; straight, gay, transsexual, asexual; Christian, Jew, pagan, Muslim, Hindu, and atheist too. Right wing, left wing, and didn't give a shit. But even this was not enough.

Nothing could convince him. Rootless, stateless, Dee Dee had moved around so much as a child, he now struggled between the artist's desire for freedom and a need for stability. Dee Dee broke the rules and won. In the process he opened the doors for millions. Who knows, maybe he had a bad night's sleep, paranoia from whatever drugs, or just bad brain chemistry. At the core of addiction is that relentless feeling of not belonging to the human race, of being different, incomplete, not good enough, or else too good for the world—Arrogant Doormat Syndrome.

"Born to Die in Berlin" (written with John Carco) describes a place I never want to be. It's a dark place involving taxicabs, cocaine, orchids. Dee Dee's words recall the secrecy and underhanded dealings, that misery roll of active addiction. In an eerie stanza Dee Dee delivers over the phone in German, recorded by Joey at home, we're resigned to a cold Berlin winter, dying among white flowers, so disengaged from others that they'll have to read about it in the newspapers.

When it comes to dope songs, Johnny Thunders's opus "So Alone" is a crushing narrative about the loneliness of addiction and the inability to find or feel love. In contrast, Lou Reed's classic "Heroin" grasps at life, defiant from the first rush of godlike glory, just like Jesus's son, transcending all. Reed reminds the profane world how lucky it is that the addict's murderous rage is contained by this anodyne solution. "Chinese Rocks" is a 1977 Heartbreakers song Dee Dee co-wrote with Richard Hell, only to have it rejected by straightedge Johnny Ramone for its unsavory druggie references. As the punk community became increasingly immersed in too much junkie business, Johnny didn't want Dee Dee hanging out with Hell, Thunders, and Nolan, who with

Dee Dee made up New York Punk's Heroin Aristocracy. Saying you got high with Thunders was high status in the scene. The Heartbreakers' "loser rock" and styling were untouchable, but those nasty habits posed a lethal threat to the Mission.

In 1980 the Ramones' version of the song was released on *End of the Century*. It speaks to the lunacy of addict life—the hapless girlfriend crying in the shower stall, everything we own being in hock, and still all we want is to go cop some Chinese Rocks. The endless drama, you're losing ground, feeling sick, but you're still rooted in the world. You're young, you've got people to run with; getting high is still an adventure, it's exciting, a wild ride.

In contrast, "Born to Die in Berlin" is narrative of addiction at the end of the line, a Wagnerian tragedy delivered with a hard crunch. Irritable, restless, and discontented; feelings of existential separateness, anxious apartness, persist; nothing can fill the hole. A rapacious creditor, dope has you now; all that's left is a solitary death march, slow, passive suicide. You feel like screaming, and you know you can't win. A sober priest once told me, "Every addict fights the devil every day to keep his soul." Dee Dee, Johnny, and Jerry were part of punk's doomed heroin posse; like Sid, they died too young. Lou Reed left this world a clean and sober man.

There are several types of alienation. *Personally*, we are alienated from ourselves. *Socially*, we are alienated from others. *Politically*, we feel invisible, helpless, and powerless. *Economically*, we're estranged from the processes and products of our own labor. *Existentially*, we are alienated from the world. *Spiritually*, we are disconnected from source/god. Entire bodies of literature in social science, twelve-step recovery, the arts, and theology have addressed the devastating impact of alienation and isolation on the inner life of the individual. Disconnectedness is linked to active addiction, homicide, suicide, serial killing, mass shooting—the outcast's swan song. Alienation is a killing floor, especially for young people.

The Ramones offered armies of loners and outsiders a road map for inclusion. As artists, they rooted through the nooks and crannies of personal experience with keen observational skills. As individuals, having lived in the dark side of the soul, they took everything that sucked then turned it into a celebration of life. There was something of a chemical attraction, as Joey once put it, among such people. Stunted, blacklisted, the "No Future" people are described by Danny Fields as the Ramones' legacy.

Once I asked C.J. what his favorite Ramones song was. "'Outsider,'" he said, "because I am. I always felt like an outsider, even when I was with the misfits of my town. Not sure why, I just never fit in." As an adult, Christopher Joseph Ward is passionately engaged in the world doing everything an individual needs to do to buffer against alienation. The Long Island father of three is a devoted family man married to an attorney with a social work degree; she's also a longtime youth advocate. Community minded, C.J. coordinates ongoing fundraisers for kids, veterans, and first responders. He's a successful touring musician, he records new music—and he's a Ramone! Still, C.J. feels like an outsider, outside of everything. "Outsider" is Dee Dee's 1983 official declaration of disconnectedness. The outsider feels put down; everything and everyone presses in on him as if he's nothing and nobody. If "Blitzkrieg Bop" raised rock and roll from the graveyards of popular culture, "Outsider" was the Ramones' credo.

When I interviewed Joey for the *Village Voice* in 1996, he explained the special connection shared by the Ramones and their fans. "The Ramones are there for all the outcasts," he said. "Alienation was definitely a feeling we went through in the early stages of the band. We were outsiders, loners. Okay, this is me, I'm myself, I'm an individual, I don't want to be like you, I wanna be who I am."

Interviewed for Monte Melnick's memoir, Joey reiterated the feeling of being an outsider, a loner. "I was a misfit. . . . I didn't get along with other kids. I didn't like Queens 'cause it wasn't me. I only had a couple of friends and I didn't fit in." He was shy and quiet, an easy target for bullies. "The greasers always looked to kick my ass." As he grew older, Joey was the kid your parents warned you to stay away from—tall, skinny, scary looking; he always stuck out. Joey said, "When you're a kid, anything that's going to set you apart makes it hard on your life." An outcast but never a loser, Joey moved awkwardly through the streets of Forest Hills. He talked *strange*, was artistic and deeply into music —that was enough to seal his fate.

Among Ramones fans, it was Joey who would become our bodhisattva—an ascended master who returns to earth in human form to teach others. A role model for kids who feel cast aside, Joey is proof that you can win in the end, and that you're good, and beautiful, no matter what people say. "There was something about the way he looked at us from the stage," says Jean, a life-long fan and suburban mother of three. "Just hearing his voice made you feel loved." The Ramones offered their followers something real and true, something to believe in as everything was beginning to crack—inside and out. And if you weren't slamming through the dark night of the soul on that particular day, hey, no worries, you just hung out and enjoyed the music.

Alienation has a positive side too, imparting a critical edge, a distanced objectivity indispensable to any writer, social scientist, or artist. Growing up absurd, the Ramones created narratives that allowed them (and us) to explore creepy feelings set to upbeat pop tunes. Nonthreatening, never getting whiney or preachy, they gently spoon-fed us. "I Can't Make It on Time" is a soulful expression of something we share just being human—feeling somehow inadequate, like we're falling short, less-than, unprepared. We're not perfect, so what? We're human, forgiven; the Ramones welcome us home, no shame, no blame. Alone or at a show, whirling, purging in a tribal sweat lodge, lights and leather: before you catch your next breath, the Ramones hit you with another song.

As baby boomers growing up watching *I Spy*, *Mission Impossible*, and *Get Smart* on TV, the Ramones brought our childhood superheroes and bogeymen back to life. In "KKK Took My Baby Away," the protagonist is frantic; they've kidnapped his girlfriend, and now he's begging the FBI to call so he can find out if she's alive. Many fans and critics assumed Joey wrote the song after right-wing Johnny stole his fiancée, Linda, from him. Monte urges us to listen closely to the words. Others insist it's about a girlfriend Joey met in the mental hospital who mysteriously disappeared one day. Either way, Johnny loved the song, didn't care what it was about; the Ramones Mission always came first.

In "Havana Affair," the Ramones penned their own spy movie about a Cuban guy who made a living picking bananas. Now he's working for the CIA, busy spying on a television game show. Let us pause to salute that song's slick baby-baby-loco-mambo refrain, the cheering for Havana, for the USA—teasing us into a festive mood. In "Sheena Is a Punk Rocker," the kids are ready to party, incongruously, heading out to the disco with surfboards in hand. But not Sheena. She's answering to a higher call; she's a dissenter, a punk rock girl. Over the bridge to Rockaway Beach, fun awaits at New York City's legendary surf city, the largest urban beach in America. It's sunny and we're busy chomping out a rhythm on a wad of bubblegum. We are way past surf music now. People who personally annoy the Ramones get theirs, too: Jackie the punk, Judy the runt, two juvenile delinquents who split to Berlin, and somehow the Ice Capades and the SLA are involved. At the very end Joey subverts the little pop tune by speculating that perhaps they'll die! But they don't. *End of the Century* brought "The Return of Jackie and Judy." They show up in New York; they're getting drunk at the infamous Mudd Club. Now a bookie and a loan shark respectively, Judy and Jackie return home just to see the Ramones.

Comic book stories filled with daytime dilemmas, acronyms, pharmaceutical monikers, and images that tickle. While the Ramones have given glue sniffing its proper due, they created a controversy with the song "Carbona Not Glue." The record company refused to release the song for many years. Then the Carbona company suits threatened to sue them over trademark violations. But the Ramones' declaration in favor of cleaning-fluid fumes caused quite a stir in the solvent-abuse community. In the end, da bruddahs swore they never did it. Well, not that much, they said. Not like you'd think. According to Joey, some of the Ramones sniffed glue in high school because it was a cheap high. Disgusted with the public outcry, Dee Dee claimed he swore it off in the eighth grade. You can hear the influence of Carbona and glue in their songs. Edgy like speed, intense but hallucinogenic, glue wipes the floor with hippie drugs like acid and pot; it renders cocaine pedestrian. Can you imagine David Byrne tripping the holy buzzwheel?

Tales of brains jammed from mainlining glue aside, the Ramones' huffing ballads were never meant as encomiums to brain damage. By the time they wrote the song, the Ramones were pretty sure nobody was doing it anymore—it was just a goof. "Now I Wanna Sniff Some Glue" was ultimately about teenage boredom, while "Carbona Not Glue" was a rant against household chemical toxicity. Of course the song was grossly misunderstood by the mainstream, demonized much like Ozzy's poignant anti-alcoholism eulogy, "Suicide Solution," which got blamed for triggering metal kids to kill themselves in the 1980s. Heartbroken over loss, Ozzy wrote "Suicide Solution" in memory of AC/DC's Bon Scott, who had died of the disease. Adult moral panic over popular culture strengthens youth alienation.

The Ramones' slapstick critique "Psychotherapy" humorously slams an entire paradigm as a crime against individuality, a velvet-gloved form of social control calculated to suppress uniqueness, originality, and creativity—every single thing the Ramones stood for. What a relief for all the kids remanded on a daily basis to some rusty-nut shrink or school counselor, only to end up feeling even more horrible. We can see how therapeutic one night of the Ramones on rotation can be for kids trapped in these psychic gulags.

The fact that uncooperative kids are routinely misdiagnosed, overmedicated, picked apart by "experts," terminally labeled defective, and condemned to bad lives made psychotherapy a perfect foil for the Ramones. DSM-5 is itself a great name for a band. But reading the fifth edition of the American Psychiatric Association's *Diagnostic and Statistical Manual of Mental Disorders* aloud, we can only imagine what the Ramones would do with those "lyrics": right up there with party tunes like "Lobotomy," "Pinhead," "Wart Hog," "Cretin Hop," and "Shock Treatment." The Ramones made a fetish out of deviance.

Dee Dee and Joey had their share of mental health professionals probing their inner lives. The result: silly songs about a kid going off, killing his family; he's mental, mental! What fun to call out the creeps, render them ludicrous, hence powerless. Bob Marley advised the people to emancipate themselves from mental slavery. This was the first step in consciousness raising. Instead of being stuck alone in some dismal institutional office, convinced you were a loser, the Ramones sat there with you making fun of the whole thing. Their rants prefigured radical psychiatrist Peter R. Breggin's blistering exposés of Ritalin and Prozac.

Without ever being pedantic, Ramones narratives also addressed central concepts in sociological thought, such as deviance and social control, labeling theory, alienation, anomie, isolation, marginality, and negative sanctions. They took the human condition very seriously, and then they pissed all over it. As we know, in commercial culture the sacred songs of the human heart are routinely repackaged and resold as one more round of false promises—phony, cheesy, unsatisfying. After a while who can feel anything? Instead, kids get angry but don't know why. To survive, they withdraw, moving further away from their own humanity.

Fans responded to the Ramones' brand of truth telling galvanically. As members of "the minority of minorities," most young people are essentially poor people, dependents, powerless and without rights. Lacking legitimacy and resources, without access to economic and social opportunities, youth are simultaneously dismissed and overregulated by arbitrary and capricious adult authorities. Of course they're pissed off! Like any other disenfranchised underclass, young people develop critical faculties and alternative belief systems to keep themselves safe and sane. The Ramones' music addressed these concerns consistently and covertly but with a light touch—perfectly balanced, like their sound system.

In the critical study of youth, the "rebelliousness" reflected in rock and roll is never dismissed as silly, hormonally driven "teens" "acting out" during "stages of development." Instead, it's viewed as a howl for respect, autonomy, agency, and legitimacy. The fortunes of young people are always related to socioeconomic conditions such as stagnation—as in the exhausted, out-of-gas 1970s. As things crumbled, the Ramones activated an ethic of inclusion that was classically American: *Give us your hungry, your tired, and your poor.*

Teenage boredom is a reoccurring theme of rock and roll, especially in Ramones songs; "I Just Want to Have Something to Do" is timeless. There are reasons kids are bored, and it's not because they're lazy or spoiled. It's because the social order infantilizes them, keeps them out of full participation in life and the labor force, dismisses them as "immature," holding them hostage in the garrison state of adolescence. Sometimes, kids want to explode. Dee Dee articulates this simmering rage in "Time Bomb." Frustrated, bitter, he has one shot, one opportunity to tell the world off. And he promises to do it well, exploding in words, condemning everyone to hell. Kids who are marginal, bullied, perpetually crushed beneath the wheel can relate.

Young people have built-in bullshit detectors. The more damaged the bonds between the individual and the social world, the sharper these critical instincts may become. As fans move into the age of majority, the Ramones' music continues to enhance individuality and creative risk-taking. How many times has the mature Ramones fan sat through a tedious faculty meeting, an office party, or family soiree silently screaming the lyrics to "Cretin Hop"? Lost in adulthood responsibilities and obligations, we are welcomed back to ourselves by the Ramones' music, reminding us who we really are. The ultimate teenage music becomes a lifelong scriptural reference for the scamp in each of us.

As a single mother in her thirties living in Florida in 1989, Cindy had never heard of the Ramones. On her first date with the man she eventually married, she saw the band for the first time at Miami's 1235 Club in South Beach. "That concert changed my life forever. It was a whole different world I had no clue existed. I loved it! I wanted to be cool like them because I thought I was just a nerdy mom who loved Barry Manilow," she says. "Way different than Woodstock hippie music, and I was hooked! I saw them one more time. They had so many great songs. . . . 'Sheena Is a Punk Rocker,' 'I Want to Live,' . . . and of course, my all time favorite, 'Rockaway Beach.'"

Cindy is a Rockaway girl. That part of her had been lost along the way. Instantly, the Ramones' music helped her reclaim it. "I love those songs 'cause they bring back memories of being young, rebellious, places I lived, and just plain simple fun with their lyrics. Truly one of a kind," she says. "Kinda like the Beatles, there will never be anyone like them." Cindy's son had been a talented teenage skate punk. Now her baby grandson sports a black Ramones onesie and Grandma Cindy has a matching T-shirt. She named her puppy after Joey Ramone. Even for an adult experiencing the Ramones for the first time, it can be life-affirming.

Personally and politically, wherever we are, the Ramones' message of belongingness can sustain us throughout the life course. It's always there to remind us we're not crazy, not alone; there's a real reason we feel crappy, estranged, bored, or unsatisfied. The music wakes us up, pulls us out of a coma—"Hey, come on, let's go do something cool!"

After he retired, Joey spoke about opening up a multidimensional New York club, "Where Worlds Collide." Sadly, he didn't live to see it. But in the "Sociology Works" section of *Experience Sociology*, a 2013 McGraw-Hill textbook by Croteau and Hoynes, there is a place where worlds do collide. A profile titled "Donna Gaines and the World of Rock Music" features a photo of me standing with Joey in the back room of Continental, the downtown club that had become his post-Ramones clubhouse. Citing my book, *A Misfit Manifesto: The Sociological Memoir of a Rock and Roll Heart*, the authors note that my work demonstrates that "a sociological imagination can be a valuable skill for a misfit to possess." I can just hear Joey laughing, "Yeah, real textbook cases." But this is the Sociology of the Ramones—subculture, deviance, alienation, social control, and the social actor. Deranged and delightful.

The Ramones' early songs were celebrations and negations, an inventory of what they did or did not want to do. If *chaos* was at the heart of the Sex Pistols' narratives, *refusal* was the Ramones' earliest concern: *I don't want you, I don't want to walk around with you, I don't care.* Affirmatively, they did wanna be your boyfriend, want the airwaves, wanna dance, and wanna be well. The Ramones gave us beautiful ballads too, like "Lovely Locket Love," Tommy's "I Wanna Be Your Boyfriend," and Joey's touching, road-weary ballad, "Danny Says."

Throughout many short songs, lyrics, tropes, and narratives the Ramones took on some of the complex existential traumas most organized religions promise to relieve through faith, prayer, communion, and community. In secular society, popular culture often serves to bind, educate, and elevate the individual. The Ramones distilled the poison heart of humanity, boiled it down alchemically, dispersing it into simple, powerful catchy phrases—slogans for daily living. The music feels like Ritalin, so fast, loud, and immediate it actually calms you down; no prescriptions or side effects. Instead of chaining the youthful spirit, the Ramones urged their fans to seize it, like the airwaves, like rock-and-roll radio. The Ramones rebooted the social memory, clearing it out in a luminous blast.

As suggested by the twentieth-century French existentialist philosopher Jean-Paul Sartre long ago, one antidote to alienation is engagement. The more we're involved in the social world— our projects, our communities, and relationships—the better off we'll be. Considered by Aldous Huxley to be the most important social movement of the twentieth century, the twelve-step recovery movement (AA) was founded in the 1930s by Bill Wilson and Dr. Bob Smith, two hopeless drunks, as a way to stay sober. Regular attendance at meetings, fellowship, community, and service to the still sick and suffering alcoholic were recommended as strategies for staying off booze. Through cultivating a relationship with a "Higher Power," the alcoholic slowly reengages with life, self, and society. This concept of a higher power is loosely constructed to mean "anything that isn't you." It may include everything from soup to nuts—sociology, the ocean, your cats, the Ramones, a beloved child, or a rock lobster. It may draw from organized religion or any other spiritual practice. For the individual locked in a bottle, the goal is to *connect*.

Alienation is a consequence of living in the social world. Community is crucial for human well-being and longevity. We cannot do it alone, no matter how torturous and repulsive it may feel to engage with others. In their time and place, the Ramones of New York City offered their fans an all-access pass into what the nineteenth-century French sociologist Emile Durkheim described as *social integration*. Most of us don't even know we're alienated; we just feel remote, outside of life, looking in, nose pressed against a plate-glass window. The Ramones gave their fans a formula for survival on the threshold of adulthood in the last quarter of the American Century, when nothing made sense, when there were no clues, no choice, or difference, and nobody even seemed to notice.

....

Why the Ramones Matter 59

The Ramones Ministry was ultimately about the hidden injuries of youth, all the stuff nobody talks about. That vague sense of dread that follows us through the day, through a lifetime; unhinged, agitated, bored, I wanna be sedated—drugs, alcohol, depression, drama, or violence. Even as they grappled with it themselves, the Ramones offered the kids another way. "The band will always be in your heart," said Marky with rueful tenderness. "And I hope that when something bothers you, some part of the Ramones is there to help you."

Born in 1967 to a German immigrant family in a small West Texas town, Robin is a Generation X Ramones fan. During World War II, Robin's grandfather had worked for the propaganda ministry in Berlin. She grew up hearing "Hitler was right on the race issue" at the dinner table. She describes an unhappy childhood. "At school I was a misfit, the kid in a corner everyone made fun of." But Robin found a lifeline in rock and roll. Initially mesmerized by KISS, she says, "I started buying anything I could find on KISS; that's how I came across the August 1977 issue of Creem— KISS was on the cover. The Ramones were inside. I was ten years old. I made sure I bought or stole every issue after that."

Robin was immediately taken with punk but only knew punks from Creem's images and text. "I pinned pictures of Iggy, the Dictators, and the Dead Boys on my bedroom walls, but the Ramones were my favorite. I thought they were *perfect*. All of this happened before I heard the music, because I couldn't find their records. When I finally did, they sounded just like I'd imagined. They were perfect."

The Ramones' focus on marginality really spoke to Robin. "Punk, and the Ramones in particular, told me I had a place. The

Ramones were welcoming. I had a people. I could be a cretin, psycho, d-u-m-b. They said leave home; I took it literally. I ran away at twelve, but the police found me. I left for good at sixteen with just the clothes on my back. I made my way to Austin and was living on the street when an all-black, holiness, sacred name church took me in. I stayed with them ten years." While at the church, Robin gave up secular music, "but punk still guided me. Punk and the Gospel were not so different to me: both shined a light on the ugly, and magnified the least among us."

Today Robin claims no religious affiliation but says she lives on everything she's learned. Including the Ramones. She never saw the band live because she spent so many years being cloistered. "Instead, I visit their graves. They feel like family. Closer than blood, although I never met them."

The Ramones' songs that mean the most to Robin include "I Just Wanna Have Something to Do," because, she says, "there was nothing to do." Also, "We're a Happy Family," because it felt so very true to her. Today festive votive candles are available featuring St. Joey, St. Johnny, or St. Dee Dee, our protectors. Moving from the parasocial to the paranormal, fans across spiritual traditions will literally pray to the Ramones, crediting them with personal salvation.

Fred is an Italian Ramones fan, a musician from Siena, Italy, born in 1971. When he was a "penniless teenager" in high school, a friend slipped him a homespun Ramones tape during detention. He put the tape in his pocket and waited for the "punishment over" bell. Fred's high school experiences sound typically Ramones. "I was a stranger in that place. Some kind of proto-punk rebel in a school full of preppies, I was a hardcore guy from a modest family within a bunch of spoiled rich kids from the high society. It was like having to walk the wire on a daily basis: I did not fit there, and I was in search of a sign and waiting for an answer." Fred was already playing the bass, very badly, he says, but with the sole intent of *being against*. "Rebelling against I did not know what, in a small-minded medieval small town in Tuscany where everybody (including my parents) apparently looked and acted the same. How could I accept that without resistance?"

Fred saw only one way out: to start a band with people similar to him and write his own music—the perfect solution. Slowly sliding into a nasty and hidden binge-drinking habit, Fred says it was easy and legal in Italy to get himself drunk. "I did not fit anywhere, I did not conform; it wasn't easy to be me. At all." Fred says the architectural design of the high school itself reminded him of a prison, "masterfully converted to keep at bay the mob of adolescents who, once shut up there with their hormones and their dreams, had given up. No encouragement to find your own path, just follow orders." Fred longed for a world that was his and nobody else's. He muses, "Could the sonic attack of the four outsiders of Queens-NYC find more fertile ground?"

That day, his Ramones tape in hand, Fred says he ran from detention home, taking a long hot shower to wash off the day. As he listened to the tape, he claims, the doors of perception opened up: he heard the audience rumbling in the background, then roaring at the entrance of a band on the stage, and finally, he says, "I felt annihilated by a chord, only one, played with such a delightfully simple distortion and at the same time wicked to die, and greeted by a dry voice shouting, 'HEY . . . WE'RE THE RAMONES! THIS ONE IS CALLED 'ROCKAWAY BEACH'!" And, he recalls, "in the background, the rasping scream of Dee Dee, who threw a hoarse spit of petrol on the flame of punk that became a fire: 'ONE! TWO!! THREE!!! FOUR!!!!'" After that, says Fred, "I was no longer the same." Hearing Dee Dee's voice was a turning point. He wonders, what would be the world without the Ramones? "My world, at least."

Like Robin, Fred never had the chance to see the Ramones live, but the relationship became a living, breathing thing, something metaphysical that even a skilled ethnographer could not measure. Fred says that music was the exact sound he needed in that very moment, "and from then on, the precise kind of energy to fuel my engine." An artist and musician, now married with a child, Fred sings in a band, Great Midori, and works by day as a manager in the wine business. He's grateful for hundreds of hours spent with the Ramones, for the answers to the thousands of mood swings, the right amount of volume at the right time, the exact distortion, that frenzied pace equal to the pack of wild thoughts running around his brain, still. "I look at my GABBA GABBA HEY arm tattoo and I always smile. . . . I am happy, I am grateful, I am alive."

Terri 805 is a punk rocker from Idaho, born in 1968, a Gen X (baby bust) fan who discovered the Ramones in 1980 when cable TV kept airing *Rock 'n' Roll High School*. Her father, a military man, declined to copy it onto Beta tape, so she put a cassette recorder next to the TV and recorded the whole thing in audio. "I listened to it constantly and became indoctrinated into the Church of the Ramones." Terri recalls being "tall, skinny, geeky. . . . Joey and I had that in common." Growing up in a community of Air Force people and retirees, Terri felt she didn't belong and had no clue where she was heading.

As a teenager, Terri enjoyed reading but loved most to daydream. "I would listen to the Ramones cassette over and over and dream about writing songs, traveling the world, leaving my isolated small town, and being a ROCK AND ROLLER!" Terri recalls being teased at school, not fitting in. "I felt rebellious and in need of black leather, dark hair dye, and a sexy new moniker. Money was tight, and when I had it I spent it at the roller rink skating to the new-wave tunes, sneaking in rum to mix with Coke." She didn't get her first Ramones record until *Pleasant Dreams*. She sat at her dad's turntable with a headset blasting that album every chance she had. "We Want the Airwaves"!!! Terri says that "It's Not My Place (in the 9 to 5 world)" is still her motto.

She hoped to meet a talented musician at the local 7-11. Instead, she says, "I drifted into bad relationships, tried drugs, went to shows, and traveled to far-away Idaho towns just to buy records. I tried to overdose on seventeen aspirin when I was seventeen because of a bad relationship." Terri says she has blocks of memories she's unable to access due to possible abuse when her father was stationed in Vietnam and she lived with her mother's parents in a new town. "It didn't matter what I did, what I thought, what I created in my head. . . . The Ramones were always there, always had a song for me, never went away." Interestingly, says Terry, who now works in human services, "their songs gave me an interest in psychology, in sociology, in diversity, and in New York." Terri still hopes to make the "pilgrimage to Forest Hills, to the site of CBGB's, to Rockaway Beach." Still wrapped in depression at times, Terri says, "I continue to turn to the Ramones."

Terri finally got to meet the Ramones after a show in Isla

Vista, Idaho. "The very first time I finally got to see them, I was struck mute. I finally spit out, 'Gee Joey, you really are tall,' and was approached by Arturo Vega to follow the band to LA. My response? 'I have to work tomorrow.' Ah, what could have been? I can only continue to dream," she says.

"I found out that there were many, many others in the world who felt as I did, and so I was never alone, even when I wasn't understood. I still had my 'Church.'" Terri, born in 1968, is a punk for life; she still chops and colors her hair in purple tints —Joey's favorite color. She's also a Grand Dachshund Matriarch —the Ramones fan dog of choice—tending to her pups in the tradition put forth by Dee Dee and Kessie. "Sometimes, in my dreams, I'm hanging out with Joey and we are just talking about life and the world. He's shy, reserved, and we are both vegetarians. We're like two buddies, and it's comfortable—because we've known each other for a long time, and through our experiences we've walked the same path. And I'm still here because, like the Ramones, I haven't given up."

Meantime, here on golden pond, I'm still talking to Joey and Dee Dee on a daily basis, blasting "I Don't Care," drumming out all the bad news with "Commando" or "Havana Affair" sixteen times a day. Ramones lyrics long ago replaced the more noxious childhood dogmas pumped into my brain. The Ramones' fan is never alone, as with any higher power. Some have a friend in Jesus; others have one in the Ramones. The Beatitudes: a poster of Joey dressed as a saint, blessing us, the inscribed benediction reminding us that all good cretins go to heaven.

....

Gathered up from everyday life, giving voice to the frustrations of marginality, the Ramones stood up to all the dirty bastards we deal with on a daily basis. The Ramones armed their fans to fend off daily assaults to dignity, psychic space, and serenity. Through an obsessive embrace of all the immediate raw resources available—material and nonmaterial, sacred and profane—the Ramones extracted maximum meaning and value from everything around them, then brilliantly churned it into art. The Ramones were American masters at cranking bricolage, Queens style.

The Ramones' stories came from living deeply and fully in the world, by ultimately accepting themselves, zits and all. If they were ironic, it was instinctive; if they were postmodern, it was intuitive. Musicians don't become lifelong cultural heroes without genuinely charismatic connections to their audiences —the ability to tap into and connect with the most vital, primal collective energies. For each Ramone—Dee Dee, Joey, Johnny, Tommy, Marky, and C.J.—creativity offered a ticket out of meaninglessness and stagnation.

The Ramones began their journey on street corners, but they looked around and imagined infinite possibilities through popular culture, especially music. Where the Pistols posited an anti-Establishment critique, making brilliantly subversive use of symbols and styles, the Ramones had a different plan, as different as eating "pizza" in London is from eating a slice in New York City. The American Dream is sustained by optimism, even when nihilism is trendy. In 1980, when asked if the Ramones were a New York band, Joey replied, "I love New York, but we think of ourselves as being more of an American band." The Ramones crafted scathing critiques of life's bitter assaults on the individual, *but they loved America*. They wanted to uplift and strengthen it, never tear it down.

One thing that differentiated the Ramones from most punk bands was their politics—or lack of. Individual members held wildly differing political beliefs. Dee Dee and Johnny made up the psycho paramilitary faction of the Ramones (libertarian?). Joey's mother was an artist; Marky's father was a labor lawyer; Tommy was glad to be safe and sound in the USA. C.J. was a populist and a patriot, like most people on Long Island. Before I knew them, I figured Joey and Marky were typical New York liberals, neurotic from being all worried about the human condition. Dee Dee could care less about politics; Jesus had chosen him out of the world, and he would *render unto Caesar*.

The band members chided each other for their affiliations. Johnny's take on Joey's politics: "He's a bleeding heart." On Marky's: "A socialist!" He dismissed them both as "a pair of old hippies," the worst thing anyone could say about a Ramone! In turn, everyone condemned Johnny as a fascist. His widow, Linda, was featured on TV formally endorsing and actively campaigning for the McCain/Palin ticket. Johnny proudly displayed a signed photo of Adolph Hitler in the living room. At the very least, he was a right-wing bohemian, like the Hells Angels. An avid collector of signed photos, vintage posters, and baseball cards, Johnny *lived* to fuck with people.

Bohemians will generally eschew the Protestant work ethic beneath the spirit of capitalism. After Johnny retired, he planned to do *nothing*. "I can stay busy all day just doing nothing. I make my own rules as I go along. I think things out for myself," he explained to me. "Work is bad," he declared, a radical notion for a Republican and refreshing from someone who considered playing in a band a job, "a silly job." "Politics" à la the Clash and a hundred thousand latter-day punk bands were subordinate to a sacred tenet of the Ramones: individuality. As artists and true Americans, the Ramones' politics were rooted in the personal-social struggles of daily living, identity, agency, liberty, and above all, freedom.

The Ramones took the human condition very seriously. But until they passed away, very little was known about them as individuals. They appeared to us as *the Ramones*, monolithic, a singular entity. At one point, I was asked to interview Dee Dee at the Chelsea Hotel for the 2004 documentary *End of the Century*. He was jittery, working to get clean (again), wouldn't speak to strangers. He had to know the interviewer, to feel safe, and no, we would not be discussing anything related to 53rd & 3rd. As a matter of record, I had my last drink in January 1997, less than a year after I first interviewed the Ramones. I was bottoming out when I met them. Like any addict, I wanted more, more of everything. In that first year, knowing that Marky and Joey were sober made it a lot easier. I was afraid I'd never have fun again, but the opposite was true. The clean, sober Ramones were *the cool cats*, living creative lives, learning new things, relaxing at the clubs with a soda or fruit juice in hand. That made them powerful examples. Dee Dee too was trying, had been for years—but it was more complicated. Being cross-addicted with a "dual diagnosis" had him cornered.

Germany! Glue! Dachshunds! Queens! Our epic Chelsea Hotel hang went on for hours, including a lengthy seminar about dachshunds, our childhood pets. Dee Dee's beloved Kessie was featured in "Dee Dee and Kessie's Adventures," a comic strip in *Taking Dope*, part of a collaboration with Paul Kostabi. Dee Dee was an army brat, growing up in the 1950s with a German mother and an American father. As a young girl growing up during the war, his mother foraged for food and hid from the bombings, starving, terrified, watching dead bodies floating down the bloody rivers.

While his father was stationed in Germany, Dee Dee spent a lonely childhood combing through the ruins, obsessively collecting Nazi memorabilia and knives. He had no friends. His parents were alcoholics. They fought constantly. They hurt each other and they hurt him too.

One day in Germany, Kessie fell into a river. Dee Dee's father just stood there watching. He did nothing; he let the dog drown. Many years later, downstairs in the green room of Continental, I remember watching Dee Dee consecrate the blackboard space with graffiti, a whimsical chalk tribute to Kessie, Über Dachshund of Berlin.

At once demonic, pop savvy, feral, sweet, and silly, Dee Dee either loved you or hated you, and that could change in the course of an hour. He was a man of faith with a pure, childlike trust. Or else he was paralyzed by paranoia-the-destroyer. There was nothing in between. Childhood trauma can push people to the borderline. Douglas Colvin was a childhood trauma survivor; Dee Dee Ramone was an artist.

As his younger brother, Mickey, explains in *I Slept with Joey Ramone*, Joey was born with a birth defect caused by an undeveloped conjoined twin that had attached itself to his back. He was left with a deep scar and ongoing mental and physical health problems that left him debilitated and prone to chronic infections. Tall, rail thin, awkward, sickly, and shy, as a kid Joey endured his share of bullying and abuse. He is described by Mickey as a good, caring older brother who invited his frightened younger sibling to sleep in his bed after a nightmare; one who reassured him during their parents' bitter fighting and subsequent divorce, and again after their stepfather's sudden death in a car accident.

A curious, generous child, as a teen Joey's behavior got increasingly bizarre and he talked about suicide. After Joey attacked his beloved mother with a kitchen knife, at eighteen, the family was forced to admit him to a psychiatric ward, where he was misdiagnosed as a paranoid schizophrenic with minimal brain damage. His mother was told he would never function in society or have a normal life. Though seeing a psychiatrist helped, as Mickey notes, Joey didn't really heal until he started playing rock and roll. In and out of day treatment, frolicking with girls he met in the "loony bin," Joey drew from these experiences, incorporating them in songs. In order to be treated like a human being, Jeff Hyman had to become the rock star Joey Ramone. Of his fame, Mickey writes, "This was no fleeting occurrence that could be erased the next time some kids pointed at him and laughed." Joey felt like a freak from the get-go. He understood too well the potential for cruelty in all of us. Even as he matured, the wounding was built into his cellular memory. *I wanna be well.*

When I interviewed Joey in his apartment in 1996, our exchange went on for hours. There was something mystical and healing about finally meeting an icon you "knew" for so many years. Usually this is a major disappointment, but not with Joey. That afternoon and well into the evening we talked about everything from music to religion, childhood and family, school and spirituality. It was lighthearted and fun, although I was astonished to learn that Joey didn't eat pizza, the Holy Sacrament of the Ramones. He was off dairy now, trying to eat healthy. An accident onstage a few years earlier motivated him to get clean and sober; now he was taking better care of himself. I would later learn that he had non-Hodgkin's lymphoma.

Mickey relates a horrific scene from their childhood of their father, Noel, throwing Joey against the wall. I had spent time with Joey and Noel. One night, Mickey's band, the Rattlers, were playing down at the Maidstone Pavilion in East Hampton, where Noel spent summers with his girlfriend, Nancy. Noel didn't want to go to the show. Who knows why? He just sat there in the car, stewing. Somehow we coaxed him out, and the three Hymans were united in the serious moonlight. Noel had a trucking company. He was not an easy guy, but Joey adored him. When he died, Joey was shattered. "My dad was my whole life."

The complexities of loving parents who hurt you can take a lifetime to sort out. Mutual brokenness and trauma connected us. If you've got it, you can spot it, and you never have to explain. This was the connection Joey had with his fans. There are decals and posters of St. Joey smiling benevolently, asking us to contemplate "wwjd?" *What Would Joey Do?*

As the Ramones' principal songwriters, Joey and Dee Dee had known their share of rejection, sorrow, pain, and betrayal. Maybe that's why an army of outsiders and misfits so completely trusted the Ramones. Even now this subculture has a familial ease to it, an instant feeling of affection. You cannot fake this. Suffering can make you bitter, but it can also bring out loving-kindness and compassion.

Johnny, too, idolized his father; in his autobiography he swoons over the tough, hard-drinking, hard-working man who forced him to play baseball with a broken toe, taunting his young son, "What did I raise, a baby?" The devoted father who would wake young Johnny up out of bed to join him on double night shifts, giving him beer to sip; the tough guy who attended every baseball game and took little Johnny, all decked out in a fancy cowboy suit, to see Roy Rogers at the rodeo. The dad who tolerated his junkie son's worst behavior, who steadfastly supported Johnny during his wasted years, powerless as his only child turned into what Johnny calls a "bad, bad person."

Johnny spent many childhood hours alone while his parents worked late at their bar. He describes his macho paternal uncles sitting around the kitchen table with his dad, drinking. They hated his long hair and thought that playing music was for sissies. It sounded like something out of "53rd & 3rd," but that was Dee Dee's song. Johnny was smart, difficult, and self-contained, trying to live up to impossible standards of masculinity and class culture. As children, we love our parents even as we fear them. There's a fine line between tough love and abuse. Denial is not a river in Egypt.

When Joey was eighteen, Johnny beat the shit out of him because he showed up late for a movie. Joey had trouble being on time. Johnny was twenty-one and Joey was eighteen. In his autobiography, Marky recounts hearing Johnny shoving and smacking his girlfriend, Roxy, around their hotel room on tour. "We would hear her stumbling, bouncing off a thin wall, and then falling onto a bed and shrieking." Nobody intervened. In an interview with *Mojo*, the band's manager Danny Fields says: "I'd stand outside the dressing room. Inside you'd hear glass shattering and bodies slamming into walls." Nobody stopped it. Nobody said a word.

According to Danny, Dee Dee was terrified of Johnny because Johnny would punch him in the face, usually after a show, screaming, "You did a B-major when you should have done a C-minor." In addition to his father's heavy-handedness, as a child Johnny sustained physical abuse from the nuns. Luckily, when his mother found out, she promptly removed him from Catholic school. Later, at the military academy *he* chose to attend, Johnny describes their corporal punishments as torture. He lasted a week at a college in Florida before coming home. Sometimes a child has limited choices: be crushed, become your abuser, or find another way. It's how kids survive.

Tommy was born in Budapest, Hungary, in 1949. His parents were professional photographers, Jews who had survived the Nazis through being hidden during the war by good neighbors. Most of Tommy's extended family had been exterminated. Even the blood of genocide did not heal Europe of vicious anti-Semitism, so the family left Hungary for America during the Hungarian revolution of 1956. Tamás Erdélyi was a short, thin Jewish boy with a funny accent who was regularly, sometimes mercilessly, bullied by the other kids. A chain-smoker for many years, Tommy had a lifelong anxiety disorder.

Certainly, not all addicts are childhood trauma survivors, and not all trauma survivors become addicts. Tommy was a trauma survivor but not an addict. Marky was an alcoholic but not a trauma survivor, unless we consider the institutional abuse he describes at the hands of high school administrators and educators. The son of a longshoreman and widely respected labor arbitrator who turned labor lawyer, Marc Bell was a wiseass, a high-spirited boy who had a twin brother. A curious child, born a musician's musician, he had been taught by a strong family to question authority and think for himself. Yet Marky experienced ongoing humiliation at school, including being told he was *stupid*.

After his best friend stole his girl, Marky got into a fight. Two cops broke it up. The next day he was dragged into the dean's office at Erasmus Hall High School, where he was viciously strip-searched. Marky describes in humiliating detail being forced to stand up, face his abusers, drop his pants to his ankles, then his shorts, then his shirt. "It was like being naked in the middle of a packed auditorium," but worse. The guys were former military —navy and marine—two cops, an administrator, a gym teacher, and one kid. "They were in their late thirties and were threatened by my generation: how we looked, how we acted, and how we didn't buy into their program." They searched Marky's shoulder bag, pants, and shirt pockets; they opened his mouth wide "like a narc dentist," he says. At one point, the guy's hand brushed the inside of Marky's calf. Then they ordered him to spread his butt cheeks. They found nothing.

That night Marky told his father what happened. The usually calm, levelheaded man lost it. Marky even left out the worst of it, afraid his protective father would end up in jail for manslaughter if he heard the whole story. The next day Marky went back to the school with his dad and his two uncles, tough working-class guys, he says, especially Uncle Johnny, who'd been in a gang. According to Marky, Uncle Johnny was still a real greaser, so kicking the crap out of a cop would have been even better than busting up a teacher.

Marky's father told the assholes what they did was sick, immoral, and illegal, and if it happened again, he and his brothers would take them outside in front of the entire school and make an example of them. As Marky describes, they were shaking, they apologized, explaining the torment as part of their "get tough on drugs" policy. All kids were suspects back in the late 1960s and early 1970s, subject to endless bullshit that only served to polarize and radicalize.

Johnny and Tommy were high school graduates; Joey and Dee Dee preferred Rock & Roll High School. Marky wasn't very impressed with mandatory schooling either; he believed real-life learning happened out in the world, not in textbooks. Prior to the marines, C.J. struggled with substance abuse and couldn't wait to go into the armed forces. As patron saints for misfit youth, the Ramones never forgot who they were or where they came from, and they emerged victorious. This made them heroes to their fans.

Trauma is part of life on life's terms. It's what we do with it that counts. Dee Dee, Joey, Johnny, and Tommy were childhood trauma survivors, sometimes multiple traumas. The "creative class" of writers, musicians, artists, and dancers is especially vulnerable to addiction and bipolarity. Childhood trauma is correlated with addiction as self-medication. Through their Mission and their Ministry, the Ramones were "wounded healers," compassionate souls ministering to others through their own brokenness as trauma survivors, outsiders, and artists. Of course most Ramones fans did not grow up in hell; they were in it for the fun, the thrill and excitement of a new scene—witnessing a riveting musical revolution that promised a cultural rebellion and delivered a social movement. But the deep bond between band and fan remained paramount to the Ramones' project. As an ethical conviction, individual Ramones were friendly, patient, accessible, kind, and loving to fans. Marky said the most important thing he learned from being a Ramone was how to treat people right; "you know, don't act like a rock star, just be yourself. . . . I hate rock stars."

Accessible on punk principles, Joey explained: "Our fans played a major part in the whole thing. I remember meeting certain artists I admired and them being real obnoxious. That wasn't how I wanted to be." Johnny has said that everything the Ramones had, they owed to their fans, so of course he treated them well. The Ramones may have been notorious for treating each other like shit, but they engaged their fans with gratitude and humility. For the Ramones, this was the higher law.

Like Black Sabbath, Public Enemy, or Nirvana, the Ramones shared similar social histories with their audiences, reflecting uncomfortable social truths, forging unbreakable, visceral ties to their fan base. The Ramones' music especially inspires us to celebrate the marginality that may come from embracing individuality—making difference work for us instead of letting it destroy us. The Ramones also helped a fledgling generation soothe some of the scar tissue left behind by previous generations—the collective shame, trauma, disappointment, and sorrow passed down to us through unresolved parental histories of family violence, incest, abandonment, war, addiction, immigration; the social inequalities we suffer based on race, ethnicity, class, sex, and gender. Systematic, institutionalized exploitation remains well hidden, especially for marginal young people who may have no clue, no defined concept of otherness or oppression beyond just feeling like shit.

The sociological imagination at work in the Ramones' narratives ties the personal to the social, focusing on the individual struggle for meaning and dignity. The Ramones held out hope and an open hand without getting in your face. You can sense the optimism to the very last drop in Joey's solo album, *Don't Worry about Me*, released in 2002. Confined to his hospital bed, doomed by lymphoma, he held on to hope—"I Want My Life!" To the end, he believed "Life's a Gas" and that this is "A Wonderful World." Days before he passed, Joey refused feeding tubes, afraid they would damage his vocal chords and ruin his singing.

Faith is relational, enhanced through the performance, process, and practice of culture and community. Like the psalms and the sacred mantras, offering courage, a reprieve, a good laugh no matter what the day brings, the Ramones have a song for everything. It's possible to string together entire sentences from their song titles. *Later for the California Sun, I wanna be sedated to the sounds of Rock and Roll Radio in Rockaway Beach, high on Carbona not glue 'cause I believe in miracles. Hey, somebody put something in my drink, but no, I don't wanna walk around with you.*

Whether you were an outcast in 1964, 1994, or 2014, you knew the Ramones were talking to you. "Pinhead" sends a signal to all lost or broken kids that they have a place, a home, a haven, a new life—with the Ramones. It's here that the band lays out their social contract with their fans: the Ramones accept you, the fans accept you, you belong, you're welcomed into the fold, you're part of us. *You're not alone anymore.*

In his autobiography, Johnny explains how the Ramones made a point of booking shows in America's most isolated places, smaller towns in Tennessee or Idaho where not much was happening for the youth. "We played places like that. I liked those places," he says. "We were always out there playing, to give fans what they deserved. We rarely missed a show but we made it up if we did," especially in the smaller towns. As Joey tells Monte Melnick: "The kids in the suburbs, in the Midwest got cheated because a lot of the people didn't go there. We'd hit all the nooks and crannies, whereas a lot of the big bands only played all the 20,000 civics. We played for the people, whereas they played for the money and couldn't have cared less if the kids could dance."

In 1981 the Ramones appeared on the *Tomorrow Show*. When asked about how they related to the kids in America's small towns, Dee Dee said: "We don't really go out to the Midwest and shock anybody, we're just the same as they are. We may be a group based outta New York, but we are all from Queens, we're suburban people and we have the same problems that everyone else has in Detroit or Ohio or anywhere else and that's why the kids are relating to us." Generating new music, staying true to form, uniformly dressed, touring, performing in fixed stage positions, over time the Ramones became a stabilizing force for their fans.

There's a long, rich legacy of literature and social science dedicated to dismantling ideologies, waking people up from the trance states of racism, colonialism, or patriarchy. Youth music, too, aims at truth telling—parents drive kids nuts; school principals and teachers can be monsters; kids can be cruel; life can be meaningless, unfair, and boring; and love can be both terrifying and painful. The Ramones understood that the personal was the social, and that the reverse was also true. They took on most every aspect of brokenness society inflicts on the individual: war, family violence, mandatory schooling, addiction, mental illness, and marginality. But they did so with sarcasm, wit, and irony. Otherwise we would have slit our wrists.

That the Ramones actually imagined they could defeat corporate rock took serious New York balls. But it's also very American. Some countries actually support artists. America swallows them up alive. Constitutionally incapable of acting normal, the Ramones were outsiders, and they always told the truth. They still do. Live on DVD or vinyl, cassette tape or MP3, the Ramones extend a radical welcome. As hundreds of memoirs and generations of kids will attest, *our lives were saved by rock and roll*. In addition to rescuing rock and roll, the Ramones rescued their fans.

3

PAF

....

After meeting the Dead Boys on tour in the Midwest in 1976, Joey set up their first show at CBGB. The first cut on their second and final album, *We Have Come for Your Children*, is "Third Generation Nation." Along with the Voidoids' "Blank Generation," US punk began to define itself as a generational response in the context of post–World War II America. Raging against the predicament of young people, Dead Boys' lead vocalist Stiv Bators warns that there is no future and no past, just a graveyard coming fast.

Third Generation Nation punks were putting America on notice—they were down to kill. In the fine tradition of Iggy Pop, Bators appeared onstage with slices of bologna safety-pinned to his jacket; removing them, he blew his nose into the salty luncheon meat, devouring each one. Punk As Fuck (PAF).

As baby boomers, we grew up on tales of aspiration and struggle, of our bedraggled, immigrant grandparents who landed in New York through Ellis Island. Desperate, hungry, escaping the wastelands of the Irish potato famine, Italy's droughts, eastern Europe's poverty, pogroms, and the czar's army, the ancestors were eventually described as *white ethnics*, not quite white but an obedient labor force bound to the old ways. One foot in the golden door meant that their Americanized sons and daughters —the boomers' parents, might live freely, without fear, in relative dignity and comfort with the promise of *more*.

By the early 1950s, youth alienation *had* became a public concern, especially among nonaffluent white males. Measured by rising rates of truancy, teen sex, pregnancy, and incarceration, the original punks were bad boys and girls-gone-wrong, dropouts; violent, apathetic, delinquent, they were James Dean and Marlon Brando, but for real. In the pre-Beatles doo-wop era, New York's street-corner societies and gangs were disaffected youth who inspired the styles and sounds that filtered into the New York punk sound.

The hitters were New York's special rebel breed—our regional version of greasers, who preceded the hippies. They dominated the streets of New York's outer boroughs, where mafioso mythologies loomed large. Johnny Ramone was a hitter. So was the Heartbreakers drummer Jerry Nolan, a Brooklyn gang member who ran with the Phantom Lords. In the early 1980s, Johnny Thunders called his band Cosa Nostra. That's why everyone was afraid of New York Punks. The Ramones' too-tough-to-die, too-cool-for-the-room look and their pummeling music had deep ties to the immigrant history of New York; to its streets and the generational traumas our parents and grandparents carried.

Long before Tom Brokaw's 1998 book tribute, we understood that our parents were the Greatest Generation. Surviving the Depression, winning a "just war," returning as heroes, they got married, had kids, and built suburbia—all for us. We were to be the crown of creation, the American Dream incarnate. In the early 1950s, white suburban families especially enjoyed enhanced access to public education, affordable housing, roads, cars, TV, and mass culture. For over twenty-five years, America promised us a land of continuous growth and prosperity, unlimited upward mobility fueled by hard work. The surf was up. And then, ka-boom! Wipeout. The decade the Ramones' music broke was a turning point in the American Dream, direction south of heaven.

According to the British music author Jon Savage, as school violence in America was exploding during the early 1970s, the time was ripe for a new white pop music movement to surface. The "nothingness" young Americans felt was much harder to pin down than in England, where class differences are more clearly delineated. America promised a more equal playing field, a classless society where everyone had a shot. Good luck with that.

The 1960s, of course, brought upheaval, increasing rebellion, and disobedience; civil rights and antiwar movements, a sexual revolution, and the emergence of youth as a prominent social voice. Already a robust consumer class, and increasingly visible, young people would be hailed by progressives as harbingers of change and condemned by conservatives as spoiled brats. By the early 1970s, the earlier radical social movements were rolling but the new decade brought increasing dissent from both the left and the right—feminism, abortion rights, gay rights, busing, tax revolts, labor revolts, the Christian right. Across all categories Americans expressed a militant spirit not witnessed since World War II. Everywhere, authority was being confronted, challenged, directly and indirectly. Punk would express this agitated mood specifically and aggressively.

In *Commando*, Johnny Ramone describes a painful time between high school and age twenty, filled with the "boredom and frustration of not knowing what to do with my life." Part of the American Dream is the opportunity to be your own commando, to set your own course. Anomie is a condition of normlessness, where the social world is shifting so rapidly you have no clue who you are, where you fit in, and what you're supposed to be doing. The familiar guideposts no longer show the way. For non–college bound youth with limited options, that can be terrifying. As I argued in *Teenage Wasteland*, for white suburban kids lacking a sociopolitical consciousness to bind them, oblivious to social class, unable to identify a common, unifying cause such as racial or gender oppression, *social* problems are perceived as *personal*, not structural. Failure is internalized as a shortcoming of the individual—you're a loser!

During the 1970s, anomic drift was further compounded by rapidly changing macro-socioeconomic conditions—commodity shortages, deficits, stagnation, and unemployment. There you are, waiting at the gas pump for hours, bursting with energy, blinded by hope, ready to light up the world, and nobody bothers to tell you the sun is going down on the American Empire.

Describing his response to the Voidoids' "Blank Generation," written by his former bandmate Richard Hell, Marky Ramone explains: "These lyrics said something, they spoke for me. I spent my childhood trying to escape the rigid ways of the World War II generation." Marky notes that he wasn't really part of the Woodstock generation either. He was somewhere in between. "I couldn't exactly claim to have a plan in life. And I could imagine a lot of my friends feeling the same way." In the lexicon of Australia's seminal punks, the Saints, *stranded*.

With its discordant, disjointed, cranky, spiky imagery and rude posturing, punk music emerged as a language of dissent, an emphatic unwillingness to swallow the crap history was dishing out—from the boring music, to the crumbling institutions, to the fracturing economic landscape. But the Third Generation Nation carried yet another inescapable burden. Writing in 1985, sociologist Michael Brake explains that "subcultures try to retrieve the lost, socially cohesive elements in the parent culture; they attempt to relocate 'in an imaginary relation' the real relations which those in subcultures cannot transcend." Brake validates such formations as attempts to resolve collectively experienced problems resulting from contradictions in the social structure. Being told you have a clear shot at the American Dream as it moves increasingly out of reach is one contradiction. But the Third Generation Nation was also deeply mired in the collective parental experience of World War II. For the Ramones' music this was critical.

In our TV shows, war movies, comic books, national holidays, at the dinner table, in the classroom, our fathers' war permeated the formative experiences of childhood, defining our generational legacy. By the age of five, we'd seen the footage of the war dead, heard stories of paternal bravery and bloodshed, and felt the sorrow and deep loss—military comrades, friends, and family members. This, we understood, was the price of our freedom and prosperity. No matter what they did, our fathers were our heroes. This was part of the Ramones' emotional and artistic backdrop.

For Victor Bockris, writing in *Beat Punk*, punk music emerges as "the last great reaction to the Second World War." Punk was a *generational response*. The punks courted fascist iconography for a reason, says Bockris. "It was like, Stop telling me about the fucking war!" Punk scholarship increasingly examines the relationship between subculture and music as it relates to World War II and the Holocaust. These concerns are central to understanding the Ramones' preoccupation with militarism and Nazi themes. In almost any Ramones biography, memoir, oral history, or early press, this connection is addressed in some form or another. It's inescapable.

Considering punk's "celebration of nihilism" in *Popular Music*, cultural historian Jon Stratton understands it as "an expression of the acknowledgement of the cultural trauma that was, in the 1970's becoming known as the Holocaust." Although Hitler's destruction of European Jews in World War II had long been known as the Holocaust, Stratton argues that the blockbuster 1978 TV series *Holocaust: The Story of the Family Weiss* did more to thrust the word into common parlance than all the history books combined. And it aired across Europe and the US just as punk subculture was becoming visible. Punk evolved in the US and UK, and across the West, says Stratton, as a *precursive experience* of the cultural trauma of the Holocaust as it began to enter "the cultural consciousness of the West."

In contrast to past music scenes, New York City had many more visible Jewish practitioners of punk—artists, managers, and record company executives. Stratton and Bockris laid the groundwork for Steven Beeber's 2008 publication, *The Heebie-Jeebies at CBGB's: A Secret History of Jewish Punk*. Where Stratton believes there's more than an elective affinity between the emergence of punk and the term *Holocaust* in the American popular imagination, Beeber goes further, framing punk itself as Jewish and citing the nervous energy, humor, irony, New York origins, and preoccupation with Nazism. "No Holocaust, no punk," he proclaims. Beeber describes the early punk scene as a subculture of "outsiders who are one of us in the *shtetl* of New York." Punks, like Jews, he says, "will self-consciously identify with the sick and twisted—what Hitler called decadent." Beeber suggests that Jewish punks reconciled the Nazi hangover by making it campy, cool, and oppositional—it "scared the squares to death." Punk's appropriation of Nazi symbolism provided a much-needed dialogue with history, identity, and the parental generation. Punk, then, becomes a way for Jewish kids to deal with the tension of persistent postwar American anti-Semitism through humor. "Punk reflected the whole Jewish history of oppression, uncertainty, flight and wandering, belonging and not belonging, always being divided, being both in and out, good and bad, part and apart," says Beeber. "Jews are the ultimate outsiders."

After the war, Beeber argues, young American Jewish kids were embarrassed to be descended from a people who had "allowed" themselves to be so profoundly victimized. In the next generation, collecting Nazi memorabilia, fucking with the annihilator's most sacred symbols, was a reminder that the Jews had won.

Referring to the early synergy between Tommy, Johnny, and Dee Dee, Beeber writes, "All three considered themselves separate from the upbeat, smiley-faced world of their time." The hippie project was not equipped to grapple with the existential truths posed by an age of unfathomable horror. For the Ramones, it was time to bring the "darker, angrier truths to the surface." The nihilism of early punk lyrics, offset by its raw power, manic energy, and thrust, offered a purging, an exorcism. Into all of this, the Ramones miraculously injected humor and irony.

Between World War II and 1978 American popular culture did not address the Holocaust, though Leonard Cohen and a few others had, in poetry and song. But the Jewish child and the German child would be immersed in it, knowing it had happened, understanding that it had been objectively possible. This shattering of existential innocence, this shame and guilt, would bind Jews and Germans in the unthinkable. Cultural trauma impacts peoples around the world—Native Americans, Armenians, Greeks, Slavs, Assyrians, Rwandans, Kurds, Bosnians, Yazidis. Creativity is one place where individual and collective healing can begin.

For Stratton, punk emerges as the site of "primal transformation of cultural trauma," as a way to think about the Western way of life for the first generation after the Judeocide. In his 2017 essay "*Luftmenschen*, Golems, and Jewish Punks: On the Pop Cultural Reflection of Jewish Identity in the Post-Shoah," German cultural critic Jonas Engelmann examines Jewish artists who engaged with Nazi iconography in the early 1970s. For example, Lou Reed, born Lewis Allan Rabinowitz, shaved iron crosses into his hair. In addition to the Ramones' "Blitzkrieg Bop," the Dictators sang "Master Race Rock." Blondie's guitarist Chris Stein collected Nazi paraphernalia, and Suicide performed the Hitler salute at shows. Engelmann notes that these musicians had Jewish backgrounds and that the appropriation of Nazi symbolism played an important role. "In the case of the Ramones who can probably be regarded as the most formative and well-known New York punk band of the 1970s, this is a topic that can be traced throughout their entire band history."

Writing for the *National Review*, Carl Eric Scott identifies the Ramones as "Holocaust-haunted pop art." The particular ethnic composition of the Ramones plus their generational, historical location, imprinted in collective memory, placed them on the front lines as artists making sense of the senseless.

In his 2002 work on the impact of slavery on the formation of African American identity, Yale historian Ron Eyerman defines cultural trauma as "a dramatic loss of identity and meaning, a tear in the social fabric, affecting a group of people that has achieved some cohesion." The memory of cultural trauma may be embedded in the offspring, even when there was no firsthand witnessing of the event; there is a collective memory, a recreation through the telling of stories—what Native American peoples call "blood memories."

Moving from deep collective memory to expression, punk's emergence marks the collective confrontation with the Holocaust and its representation in pop culture and popular consciousness. Stratton describes a Western civilization reeling from the collective shock that "*apparently* civilized Europeans could engage in genocidal acts against groups of people thought by most Europeans as Europeans." This, he argues, "undermined the certainties of post-Enlightenment modernity and contributed to the sense of unsettlement of morals, ethics which characterized the experience of Post-modernity." Punk, he says, "marks a critical cultural moment in that transformation." It was a place where nihilism could be expressed. The Ramones' music was instrumental in pushing that transformative process forward.

Songs written by Joey were typically more upbeat, and he is credited with using the term "punk" for the first time in a song, "Judy Is a Punk," on the first album. In contrast Dee Dee's work tilted more toward negativity, but even in their darkest hours, addictions and dysfunctions ablaze, the Ramones never succumbed to the self-immolating nihilism that ultimately defeated the Sex Pistols. In an interview I conducted with New York singer-songwriter Raymond Jalbert, he explains the early appeal: "Kids wanted the thrill of being nihilistic and rebellious —like the Ramones." An early CBGB's scene habitué, Jalbert notes, "They invited us to explore the outer limits of culture, because we *could!*" The Ramones, he adds, were always great fun, "an outlet for misfit teenagers, a way for burned-out, wayward kids *to have fun* with nihilism, something no other music could have provided."

Some Ramones fans were *personal* trauma survivors, broken kids who identified as outcasts and misfits. Others were bored youth who viewed nihilism as edgy and cool. And many more never gave it much thought. Punk's engagement with Nazi iconography, styles, symbols, and story lines is now widely viewed as a response to, and a rejection of the parental generation's unresolved conflict and not, as some early critics feared, a rising neofascist sociopolitical agenda. The convergence of American punk as a unique musical form and the need for a generational response to the postwar permeates the Ramones' music. They emerge as America's premier punk band addressing postwar cultural trauma.

There are three types of trauma: personal, physical, and cultural. Trauma of any type can remain embedded in us—physically, psychically, and emotionally. The Fatherland was Hitler's vision of world conquest and genocide. It was the Nazi fixation, the authoritarian regime's wet dream. But there was another fatherland closer to home: the psychic graveyard of our traumatized American dads. Broken by war, untreated, self-medicating —usually with alcohol—and emotionally unstable, our fathers bore witness to the horrific truth, the boundless human capacity for hatred and cruelty. For their American children, the fatherland was the generational hangover of collective brokenness.

It was also a cultural trauma that permeated everything in New York City's outer boroughs and suburbs, especially in communities where large concentrations of returning veterans, including Jewish families, had settled—like Forest Hills, homeland of the Ramones. Except for Tommy, the son of Holocaust survivors, and C.J., whose father was a Vietnam veteran, all of the Ramones were sons of World War II veterans.

....

In his 1976 *Village Voice* Consumer Guide review of *Ramones*, Robert Christgau said: "I love this record—love it—even though I know these boys flirt with images of brutality (Nazi especially) in much the same way 'Midnight Rambler' flirts with rape. You couldn't say they condone any nasties, natch—they merely suggest that the power of their music has some fairly ominous sources and tap those sources even as they offer the suggestion. This makes me uneasy. But my theory has always been that good rock and roll should damn well make you uneasy, and the sheer pleasure of this stuff—which of course elicits howls of pain from the good old rock-and-roll crowd—is undeniable."

As premier teenage music, above all punk aims to shock the established order and empower powerless youth. What better way to rile 'em up than celebrating the Nazis, Satan, Charles Manson, gangsters, serial killers, outlaws. Stick it! According to Mickey Leigh, Johnny especially embraced these figures. For kids who want to slam it to the social order, these are the go-to guys.

"Today Your Love, Tomorrow the World," the last track on *Ramones*, is a first-person narrative of a small-town German kid who is tired of being pushed around, treated like shit. The original lyrics were changed from a proud Nazi's first-person narrative to that of a disoriented shock trooper still hell-bent on defending the Fatherland. According to Monte Melnick, Seymour Stein, the founder and president of Sire Records (the Ramones' first label), was horrified by the first incarnation of the song. "You can't do that," he said. "You can't sing about Nazis! I'm Jewish and so are all the people at the record company." Monte, Joey, and Tommy were Jewish too. Reworking the lyrics, Tommy transformed them from a glorification to a parody of Nazis. As Johnny explains in retrospect: "We never thought anything of the original line. We were being naive, though. If we had been bigger, there would have been a bigger deal made of it by the press." Ironically, for Johnny, the lack of recognition for the band likely shielded them from scandal.

George Seminara identifies "Today Your Love, Tomorrow the World" as a historical moment in popular music, when the Ramones realized the Nazis could be used as a joke. It was now okay to make fun of them. Mel Brooks had opened that door in his 1967 film, *The Producers*, and later in a Broadway musical comedy about Hitler. In a 2006 interview with Germany's *Der Spiegel*, Brooks, who is Jewish, explains, "Of course it is impossible to take revenge for six million murdered Jews. But by using the medium of comedy, we can try to rob Hitler of his posthumous power and myths."

For some, it was too soon. For others—especially the UK kids, who already had the first album and knew the song—Nazi was a brand-new punk toy. The song title itself may be a play on "Today Europe, tomorrow the world," a quote (dubiously) attributed to Hitler. More likely, given Dee Dee's war movie obsessions and his hatred of Nazis, it's a reference to the 1944 classic, *Tomorrow the World*, about a German kid named Emil, formerly a Hitler Youth. He comes to America to live with his uncle, who tries to convince him to reject Nazism. American war propaganda; the redemption of lost youth through familial love; art as a crucial step in collective healing.

Over time, punk subculture would splinter off into various factions, some to the far right, others far left. But the Ramones were never the darlings of any neofascist youth subculture. If some took their words literally, as humorless endorsements of fascism, they were already missing the point and weren't Ramones fans to begin with.

When Tommy Ramone was asked by the *New York Times* how he, a refugee from Jew-hating postwar Hungary and also a child of Holocaust survivors, felt about his bandmates' and associates' Nazi fascination, he said: "Growing up with the fear of the Holocaust, being with John and Dee Dee was like living with danger. There might have been an element of that—just as there was in my attraction to rock and roll." He explained, "It could have been that I was rebelling by hanging out with them." Tommy initially hid his Jewish identity from his bandmates. But he told

Everett True that he was also deeply disturbed by it but didn't want to censor Dee Dee's songwriting. Of the Ramones' commercial prospects Tommy concludes, "I'm sure it must have hurt us tremendously."

Joey's parents were American born. They met in the Catskills, New York's "Borscht Belt," the postwar dating and mating grounds for Jewish singles. As his close friend and journalist Rachel Felder told Ramones tour manager Monte Melnick, "Joey made it OK to be a geeky Jewish kid from New York and be a rock star." As Patti Smith Group guitarist Lenny Kaye explained to the *New York Times*, using forbidden imagery can sometimes make it your own; adding, "Punk rock really took a lot of symbols and turned them on their back." In the sociological world of "labeling theory" and "cultural resistance," punks perfected a way to *fuck shit up*: flip it. Take the demeaning label back, claim it as your own, then hurl it back, destroying it in the process—as in the reclaiming of the *N* word in hip-hop, the *Q* word in LGBTQ theory, or *B* in feminist literature. Take it home, Punk As Fuck!

Half the Ramones were Jews and the other half were obsessed with Nazi artifacts. They all grew up in New York, a city where Jewish culture, like gay culture, was more easily absorbed into popular culture. Each founding member of the Ramones embodied some aspect of his generational struggle, but none more than Dee Dee, a German American kid with a very European sensibility. He embodied punk's response to the horror —the contradictions, the personal and cultural impact of the war. In a conversation with Legs McNeil, recalling his childhood years in Pirmasens, Germany, a small town on the French border, Dee Dee explains that the German side of the border was the Siegfried Line and the French side the Maginot Line. That's where Dee Dee found the old bunkers filled with new toys—Nazi war relics, old helmets, gas masks, bayonets, and machine gun belts. After a year or so, Dee Dee started dealing war relics. "I'd always been fascinated by Nazi symbols—from finding them in the rubble in Germany. They were so glamorous. They were just so pretty," he says. "My parents were very upset by that."

One time, Dee Dee found a Luftwaffe sword; it was so beautiful, he said. He planned to keep it, or sell it for big bucks. "When I brought that home, my father got uptight and said something really sick, he said, 'Can you imagine all our guys that died because of that?' I thought, *This guy is a real asshole.* As if he really cared. I didn't figure my father for any passions like that, about anything. And from that day on, he just became a total joke to me—and I stopped fearing him." Dee Dee's band brothers knew he hated Nazis, but for Dee Dee it was more complicated. His mother grew up under a regime later declared supremely evil. His father fought to defeat it in the Battle of the Bulge. World War II and "Germany" play out over and over again in Dee Dee's art. There's a yearning for reconciliation and the resignation that it will never come. Nothing will ever make it go away or render it undone. Not the music, not love, not even the drugs.

On 1977's *Rocket to Russia*, in "It's a Long Way back to Germany," it takes Dee Dee a total of four lines to express a most debilitating loneliness, loss, and longing, waiting to reconnect, to return, a diaspora of the soul. For Dee Dee, Germany remains a central wound—his mother's loss, his lost mother, and a lost home—a part of himself forever buried in the rubble along with all the shiny German artifacts. His father's American victory is

Donna Gaines

now an occupying force, with Dee Dee foraging through the debris.

In 1950, in *The Authoritarian Personality*, the German Jewish philosopher and sociologist Theodor Adorno and others investigated the personality traits that lead to fascism. Authoritarianism is measured by the F-scale ("F" is short for "pre-fascist personality"). A major hypothesis of the study is that the authoritarian personality syndrome is predisposed to right-wing ideology and therefore receptive to control under fascist governments. The authors link this conformity to several factors, including repressed homosexuality, rigid childrearing practices, and conformity.

In "Commando," the song penned by Johnny based on his love of war movies, (and possibly the British comic book series commonly known as *Commando Comics*), we have a real warmonger, a career warrior blinded by obedience. In the cartoon video of the song, planes fly in, full formation. Drawing from *Apocalypse Now*, featuring TV character Sgt. Bilko, Alfred E. Neuman of *Mad Magazine*, and other familiar pop cult references, the Ramones lay it all out as a set of four commandments, rules that must be obeyed. First rule: we see Dee Dee, who's carefully scrutinizing a long list posted on a wall; these are the laws of Germany. Second rule: Joey hugs a little old lady, being nice to Mommy. Third rule: Johnny slips through a clandestine alley, furtively spotting Boris and Natasha. He flips them the bird and keeps walking; he won't talk to them—they're Commies! The fourth rule serves up a big fat kosher salami on a platter. The first rule (German law) is negated by the fourth (kosher salami); that is, *suck my Jewish dick*.

In the hands of the Ramones, war, the Soviet Union, spies, military maneuvers, oppressive matriarchy (Be nice!), even the horror depicted in *Apocalypse Now* become silly, slapstick, cartoonish. Otherwise, this material would have been unbearable (and too didactic to be rock and roll). Song meanings remain delightfully ambiguous, propelled by the sheer force of the music. The Ramones were not the Clash and this was not England. The Ramones operated in a very different sociohistorical context, aiming for max appeal within a larger, more reactionary dominant order. I remember Dee Dee saying that living in America was too uptight (puritan). "Europe is much looser."

Even the Ramones' reigning anthem, "Blitzkrieg Bop," had a sketchy little subtext. Originally written by Tommy as "Animal Hop," Dee Dee rewrote it, shading it with Nazi overtones. Translated as the German military word for "lightning war," "Blitzkrieg" is pinned to 1935 by sources, who define it as an intensified military campaign aimed at certain, immediate victory —not unlike the Ramones Mission. Thanks to Dee Dee, the line about shouting from the rear was changed to the more aggressive shooting in the back. With fists pumping and voices chanting a now-famous refrain, the song hints at goose-stepping, implicating both national socialism and disco's glossy conformity and regimented line dancing. The Ramones are calling us to arms as they rail against the rigid obedience to rules that makes fascism possible. They put all that together in their debut single, as the first cut on their first album. We begin to comprehend both their artistic brilliance and their cultural importance.

At a time when American intellectuals were turning away from the social world, increasingly buried in the minutiae of "the text," the Ramones demonstrated more guts than anyone by calling out President Reagan in "Bonzo Goes to Bitburg (My Brain Is Hanging Upside Down)." Reagan's 1985 tour of Germany's war dead, including the graves of forty-nine Nazi ss soldiers, made songwriters Joey and Dee Dee sick. Like it was nothing, like he was going out for tea. Unexpectedly, the "apolitical/antipolitical" Ramones stepped up, but not without a struggle.

Like most Republicans, Johnny idolized Ronald Reagan. He initially made the band change the song title from "Bonzo Goes to Bitburg" to the more value-neutral "My Brain Is Hanging Upside Down." Eyes fixed on the Mission, Johnny also feared alienating fans (and mediators) by taking sides against a popular president. Still, when most remained silent, the Ramones spoke out. Issued as a UK single in 1985, later released on *Animal Boy* in 1986, eventually the song's full title incorporated both versions. In his review of the album for *Spin*, and of "Bonzo Goes to Bitburg (My Brain Is Hanging Upside Down)," John Leland applauds the Ramones' astute instinct for tapping into public sentiments. "Just listen to Johnny's freight cars of guitar chords, Dee Dee's 'ahh, naa naa naa' surf harmonies, and Joey's down-to-earth irritation at watching our commander in chief on TV. The Ramones are so brilliant because they perceive the world the way regular people do—through television."

By the late 1970s and early 1980s America's punk and hardcore scenes would become prime combat zones between antiracist punks, skins, and neo-Nazis. Punk music continued to evolve, and by 1986 scene violence between punks and skins was so bad that Tim Yohanan, the late editor of seminal San Francisco hardcore zine *Maximum Rocknroll*, asked me to write an educational essay about it. In "Night Rally: Youth and Fascism Today," I call for scene unity and recognition of the common struggles all young people share as the minority of minorities. Three decades later, punks and Nazis are still fighting on the streets from Berlin to the UK, from the USA to Denmark and France.

Antifa has its roots in Anti-Fascist Action from European political movements in the 1920s and 1930s, when militant leftists battled fascists in the streets of Germany, Italy, and Spain. After World War II, as fascism faded, so did early Antifa. After the Berlin Wall fell, neo-Nazism resurfaced in Germany. Young leftists, anarchists, and punk fans responded with street-level antifascism.

After Charlottesville, writing for the *Atlantic* in 2017, Peter Beinart explained the relationship between the early Antifa movements and American punks. "In the late '80s, left-wing punk fans in the United States began following suit, though they initially called their groups Anti-Racist Action, on the theory that Americans would be more familiar with fighting racism than fascism." Known for militant protest tactics, including property damage and physical violence, according to Beinart, antiracist activists toured with popular alternative bands in the 1990s, trying to ensure that neo-Nazis did not infiltrate the scene to recruit their fans.

The Ramones were antiauthoritarian to the core. We see this in their personalities, values, imagery, and narrative concerns, in their songs of refusal and celebrations of individualism. In "I'm against It," Joey doesn't even like Burger King—he doesn't like anything! Though some of Johnny's comments and his bullying actions bordered on the authoritarian, he was fiercely individualistic; so were each of the Ramones, as artists and as people. That extraordinarily discordant chemistry is what made them the Ramones.

Individualism is itself a core American value. Maybe *the* core American value. It promises freedom, liberty, and the pursuit of happiness—as we define it. Johnny's youthful anomie was healed by his dedication to his music, his mission, and his band. The Ramones' material remained focused on the rights of the individual and the power of an oppositional subculture to protect them. For Antifa, so deeply rooted in America's early punk and hardcore subcultures, authoritarianism is the ultimate enemy, the foundation of fascism itself. Individualism is incompatible with authoritarianism—left or right. If Dee Dee struggled with the competing claims on his soul by Germany and America, Johnny's private war was between his artistic need for individualism versus an ingrained authoritarianism. Joey loved cats.

At every turn the Ramones were busy undermining authority, sabotaging meaning, imparting survival strategies, and neutralizing enemies. They ultimately succeeded in making Nazis look idiotic and ridiculous, like cartoon characters. Postwar, post-Holocaust, the great scary bullies of history emerge in their songs as psychos, seething maniacs, delusional jerks, and pasty losers cranked on crystal meth—the ss drug of choice. Hitler youth emerge as tragic youth, duped by yet anther false messiah, drunk on broken promises and dead-end ideologies, the damned. It's mostly the young who fight the wars, and never the fortunate sons or daughters. The Ramones' project propelled the Third Generation Nation forward, rode them out of the Fatherland, glider-riders for rock and roll.

"Todos somos Ramoneros!" Victor Bockris viewed early punk as a rejection of the relentless preoccupation with Nazism imposed upon the postwar generation. After their defeat, former Nazis found comfort in exile-friendly Argentina and Brazil, two countries where the Ramones are as revered as the Beatles are in the USA. Their appeal to two generations of fans, especially in Argentina, remains massive; both C.J. and Marky tour there regularly. In *Raw*, the Ramones' DVD based on home movies Marky took on tour, their Argentine fans go bonkers. In addition to riotous backstage banter, the documentary reveals riveting images of rabid fans stalking the Ramones, rocking their van, flooding the streets in regulation band T-shirts and leather jackets, mobbing their idols, and being hysterical, like fans in the Beatles' first tour of the USA. The Ramones had to be sequestered at their hotel, though crafty fans found ways to smuggle in special treats for Dee Dee. Marky kept recording, C.J. slipped downstairs to talk to girls, Joey chilled, and Johnny stayed locked in his room playing video games.

In March 1996 the Ramones played a farewell concert to forty-five thousand fans at the River Plate Stadium in Buenos Aires in what was to be their last international performance. Writing from Buenos Aires, Will Lamborn explains that the Ramones had built such a fiercely dedicated fan base that a major Buenos Aires daily paper branded them the "Argentine Punk Band—La Banda Punk Argentina." Lamborn attributes the Ramones' appeal as "an unusual sort of chemistry and mutual appreciation developed over the course of eight visits to Argentina in nine years that accumulated twenty-seven of the Ramones' 2,263 lifetime concerts."

The first tour was in 1987. By 1996, Lamborn says, "Argentina had become 'Ramonesland,' and their fans, 'Los Ramoneros,' could be frequently spotted roaming the streets of Buenos Aires." It was in Argentina that Dee Dee met his wife, Barbara, in 1997. A teenage Ramones fan, she grew up with posters of her idol and future husband plastered all over her bedroom walls.

Back then, in 1987, Joey said he had no idea what to expect from the first Argentine tour. Built in 1978, Obras Sanitarias Stadium in Buenos Ares was filled to capacity with four thousand fans for the first concert. Lamborn notes that the concert was so successful it led to a three-night stand in the same venue in 1991. By 1992 and 1993, this expanded to five nights. The size of the venue grew as the band's following increased. By 1994 the Ramones required an even larger venue. In keeping with their commitment to isolated kids in far-off places where access to music is limited, the Ramones returned to Argentina a few months later specifically to tour through the interior provinces.

In October 1995 the Ramones played six sold-out nights, returning in 1996 for the final tour. Lamborn points out that the source of the Ramones' ongoing romance with the Argentine public remains unclear, noting that the groups with the largest followings have been the mainstream megagroups, such as U2, the Rolling Stones, Queen, and oddly, Oasis.

Assessing the Ramones-Argentina relationship, Lamborn suspects that Argentine music fans' seeking release from the harsh realities of ongoing economic crises allowed them to identify with "the stripped down rock played by four average guys sporting uniform leather jackets and jeans." Regardless, he says, "La Banda Punk Argentina (from New York)" had carved out a niche in Buenos Aires, instigating a new urban youth subculture. The Ramones' endless touring of Argentina earned them the status of the American band with the most visits to that country.

Marky describes South America as the Ramones' home—the band greeted like returning conquerors, thousands of stadium fans crowd-surfing the shows, kids as young as ten in the audience, everyone chanting "Hey ho, let's go," demanding more encores. In his book he describes Argentina as a class-conscious society with a centuries-old caste system, to which the Ramones might have represented a level playing field, especially for its nonaffluent young people. "All you needed were sneakers, jeans, a t-shirt and leather jacket and you were one of us." Membership, he says, wasn't free, but it was cheap.

Historically and by all accounts, Argentina, in addition to harboring exiled Nazis, boasted one of the most oppressive military regimes. At any time you could be "disappeared." This theme continues to permeate Argentine art and cinema. During the early 1970s, as government censorship intensified, radio shows were canceled, stations were nationalized, and there was no music for the kids. By the 1980s, with the return of democracy, that changed; rock and roll flourished and the Ramones seized the day.

As Marky explains, Argentina's kids had spent most of their lives dealing with shitty governments, jobs, and surroundings. "A rock show is a short, but huge relief, from reality, sending a booming message to authority," he writes. For the kids, a good rock band offered antiheroes. The Ramones' street look, he says, plus their raucous, "obnoxious songs, no-bullshit stage presence," made them perfect role models for disaffected youth.

"I believe the kids in South America saw the Ramones as

rebel spirits, unconventional and related to them in that way," says Monte in our interview. The tour manager also points out that promoters in Argentina paid them well, got the Ramones tons of airplay (something the assholes in the USA couldn't be bothered to do), and flew them in first class. As Arturo Vega told Everett True, building a following in Argentina took ten years, and by 1995 the Ramones' shows outsold the Rolling Stones. He also adds, "The Argentinean promoters had TV and radio, but you can only promote a band so much. The insanity they provoked in people could not be implanted."

It was the Ramones fans from Argentina and Brazil who reflected back the love and loyalty the band so freely bestowed. On April 24, 2001, the Ramones' career anthology, *Hey! Ho! Let's Go*, was certified platinum in Argentina, selling more than forty thousand copies. To date, this is the only platinum record the band has ever received.

....

DIY. At a time when traditional avenues to success were blocked for most American kids, the Ramones demonstrated how to construct an alternative economy for the production and consumption of music. They successfully modeled DIY (do it yourself) creativity for millions. The kids had an alternative paradigm that offered opportunity, agency, and a new economic organizational model. In the local economy of the scene, DIY was foundational. It was a creative response to nonaffluent youths' lack of access, power, and material resources. Rock and roll has always offered kids a free space to reinvent themselves. The creation of a subculture is a communal effort.

Oppositional subcultures especially help kids find and build community. Active engagement in community heals alienation. Music-based deviant subcultures offer especially valuable social support for alienated youth. The punk scene in the late 1970s was surely that.

Over forty years later, America's runaway and throwaway kids—homeless "gutter" punks, street kids in Mohawks, leathers, dreadlocks, with piercings, facial tattoos, and chains—still find meaning, community, wisdom, and safety zones in punk. Along with heavy metal, and hip-hop scenes, punk continues to offer young people a road map, and a guide to meaningful career opportunities.

Reflecting back on his first encounter with television's "Johnny Jewel," Jon Savage tells *New York Magazine* writer Mark Jacobson: "I was a young man coming out into the world. I thought the world was fucked, I needed something to show me the way through this, and what worked was the music." He went on to become one of England's most accomplished music writers. Immersion in punk opened up career paths for many of us —as writers, stylists, producers, professors, and entrepreneurs.

To be sure, the punks did not invent DIY; it's been around for centuries. Born out of economic necessity and an ideology of self-sufficiency, with the goal of autonomy and independence from consumer society, the DIY ethic eliminates the middleman. It rejects the expert and reclaims the means of production from the corporate entity. Kids become their own hair stylist, publisher, music label, producer, designer, publicist, blogger, public relations firm, or agent. In the late 1940s, the early Rockaway Beach surfers used ironing boards and diving suits before the

Aloha practice became an international sport and multimillion dollar industry. California's original skate punks nailed roller-skate wheels on to plywood and let it rip on LA's city streets. DIY praxis requires learning, tinkering, experimenting—creativity and invention. It fosters a degree of economic independence as well as thrift, and it has a spiritual component as well: recycling and reimagining found materials in new ways without wasteful, wanton destruction of the ecology.

The original punks published street sheets, fanzines, and comics, drawing them on available paper, reproducing them at the library or better yet, on the fly at work, then distributing them to help build the scene. Cut your own hair; make your own clothes; release your music on homespun labels using living-room studio equipment; create and distribute flyers to adver-tise your shows; organize tours; negotiate gigs; and generate the merchandise to support your band. DIY identities followed, like the Ramones, and band names became surnames, a new family.

DIY remains foundational to punk populism, celebrating manual labor or skilled craftsmanship, exalting the individual who seeks out applied knowledge and expertise. DIY empowered the punk scene at the individual and collective levels, identify-ing and applying alternative approaches. A core contention of DIY ideology is that nonaffluent, average kids are valued creators of culture with the right to express and produce important work. This is a radical response to the cultural hegemony of the 1970s and remains a critical element in youth culture. It's also a goal among a new generation of radical educators.

The Ramones created their empire on DIY technologies as a bunch of neighborhood guys with no cash flow, limited support, and a load of raw talent. They created an industry, and we were part of it. Monte learned how to manage tours; Joey and Dee Dee learned how to write songs, and perform them; Johnny learned how to market and sustain an image; Marky learned how to rebuild cars, make movies, and brand his own pasta sauce. Tommy learned how to promote and produce a new, unique musical form. Arturo, originally a roadie, was a fine artist who learned how to design band logos, master stage lighting, and innovate iconic T-shirt designs.

Joey never wavered in his commitment to punk ethics, to DIY, the local scene, punk subculture, or the Ramones Mission to protect rock and roll and serve the fans. As the Ramones said, New York City really has it all. Well, once upon a time that was actually true, mainly because Joey Ramone lived there. After the Ramones retired and until his death in 2001, Joey ruled the Post-Ramones Empire of NYC. He loved to stroll along St. Mark's Place enjoying a coffee, grabbing cookies at the Black Hound bakery, scarfing down pumpkin ravioli at Danal. He favored Veselka, vegan meals at the Angelica Kitchen, most of all sushi at Hisaki. The East Village was Joey's neighborhood. Before he retired, he kept the local punk scene lively by putting together a series of quirky, cool, sold-out extravaganzas. After, he devoted himself to it wholeheartedly, hosting shows across the street from his apartment at the legendary punk palace, Continental. By 1996, thanks to wise stock market investments, Joey Ramone was a millionaire who owned property and enjoyed fine dining. But he was still *Joey*.

By 1996 Dee Dee was surfing the wild winds and Johnny had moved to LA. Tommy still lived in Queens but was mostly upstate with his lifelong partner, Claudia Tiernan, working on their bluegrass-country band, Uncle Monk. Marky was in Brooklyn and C.J. on Long Island, though each one was often on tour with his new band, stopping by to play locally whenever he was in town.

In *Please Kill Me*, McNeil and McCain's classic, uncensored oral history of punk, the authors map out the who, how, and where of seminal NYC Punk's scene. Starting with less than zero, the NYC scene was built from the street up, like hip-hop; no corporate sponsorship or mainstream support, and young people doing it for themselves. Like punk scenes around the world, the original NYC scene was self-sufficient, local, loosely organized, unprofessional, antibureaucratic, and at least in spirit, nonhierarchical.

Through DIY and the local economy of the scene, punk subculture emerged. The Ramones were at the forefront of this, promoting the ethical convictions of DIY punk with rigor and determination, retaining purity long after others had mainstreamed, sold out, or died out. In 2005, after losing the twin towers, three Ramones, and most of our clubs to the gentrification that gobbled up Manhattan real estate, CBGB lost its lease and the club closed its doors. Our city was gone. The surviving Ramones continued to record and tour, supporting, producing, and nurturing new bands, keeping hope alive. It was the end of an era. But the movement the Ramones had envisioned, the values they embodied, would outlive them, the clubs, the scene, even the city that spawned them.

4

The Good, the Bad, and the Ugly

....

Hanging out with a Ramone wasn't much different from listening to their music—like living in a comic strip. Once Joey and I went out for pasta and ordered a sick dessert called the *fonduta*. It was fresh fruit you'd dip into a chocolate sauce, like fondue. We had to order it because it was so go-go boots and Laugh-In. It was totally gross; we could barely swallow it. But I couldn't stop saying, "Fonduta! Fonduta!" I drove him insane with my high-pitched bleating. Joey could be extremely good-natured. He'd just laugh and call me "a nut job." Like me, Joey didn't cook. He also had a wicked sweet tooth, so we often got into trouble together, especially at the movies. We ate way too much candy, and if Joey liked the film, we'd have to see the movie twice.

Joey adored kids and wanted to get married. He doted on his goddaughter Millie and girlfriend Angela's daughter Raven. But his illness was increasingly overwhelming, and he didn't want to drag anyone into it. Joey loved to sit around for hours watching Maria Bartiromo talk stocks on TV. According to the *Guardian*, when the popular CNBC financial analyst started getting e-mails from Joey Ramone in 1998, she ignored them, assuming he was just some weirdo. But Joey was looking for investment advice. "I started getting emails from him and he would say 'Maria, what do you think about Intel or what do you think about AOL' and I thought who is this person emailing me? It's crazy, he's calling himself Joey Ramone." Over time, they became friends. Joey was very attuned to the markets, says Bartiromo. "He really understood his own investment portfolio. Joey Ramone was a fantastic investor." He also had a massive crush and even wrote a tribute for her, "Maria Bartiromo." At one point the network invited Joey to perform the song on the floor of the New York Stock Exchange, but he declined—an acoustic set just wouldn't cut it. "Maria Bartiromo" was later released on Joey's solo album, *Don't Worry about Me*, after his death in 2001.

A simple phone call with Joey could easily turn into a seven-hour deal because he had call waiting. You'd be deep into it, and then his broker would call. Or his lawyer, or Daniel Rey, or his mother, or some girl he met in Japan. He would ask you to please hold, and then he'd forget. So you'd call back, and he'd do the exact same thing to the other person. It was easy to spend a whole day on the phone with Joey.

I spent long afternoons with Joey poolside in East Hampton at his dad's girlfriend's condo. Dressed in our ratty surf-rocker clothes, situated among the demure senior citizens, we felt like retirees in Miami Beach in the 1950s. We ate deli while Noel and Joey fought ruthless games of checkers. Noel always won, Joey always demanded a rematch. One night when Joey and I went out to Gosman's for lobsters, some kids slipped out of the kitchen and followed us out through the streets of Montauk. Accelerating their pace, gaining momentum, they caught up to us. I got edgy; we were alone, and it was dark, isolated. But I'd forgotten who he was—the kids just wanted his autograph. As we drove down Montauk Highway, "Stairway to Heaven" came on the radio and we harmonized. Well, Joey did. I squawked along.

Joey had a nickname for me, "Dieter," after Dieter Zetsche, the German president and CEO of Daimler Chrysler. From then on I was "Dieter Dymer-Chrysler." Joey never called me Donna again. "Dieter!" He liked the way it sounded. Sometimes he visited me in Springs, an arty fishing enclave in East Hampton where I shared a summer home with pals from the *Voice*. Mornings we'd scarf down homemade blueberry muffins and coffee, making the scene at the Springs General Store. Evenings we'd stroll through the Village, pre-Starbucks, with Joey, a stockholder, searching in vain for a decent cappuccino. Stopping in at the galleries, making fun of the bad art, watching the people, checking movie listings. By day we'd hang at Main Beach, checking the scene and the surf.

The house was on Gerard Drive, on the water, and Joey loved swimming in the backyard—"Bonac Creek" (Accabonac Harbor). One day, while I was underwater diving for mudpack material, I heard Joey's voice. "Uh, Donna, I'm stuck. I can't get my foot out of the mud." We were boroughs kids, terrified of the elements. Rats and roaches we could handle, but oozing gypsy moth carcasses splattered on the deck? Forget it. When Joey finally wrestled free, his sand sock was gone, buried deep in the muck. I tried to retrieve it, snorkeling the creek, mud diving for hours, but it had disappeared. The next day, the sand sock had mysteriously washed up on shore and there it was, under a tree. The neighbor, a local bay man, had fished it out.

A fiend for details, Joey knew the answer to any obscure pop culture question you could dream up. Like, who wrote that song on which label? Who did backup vocals? And what style of clothes were we wearing when the song hit the charts? Then he correlated all this with our favorite TV shows for that year and what drugs we were taking. And then he'd rattle off his five stock picks of the week. He was open to any kind of music, and we especially enjoyed AC/DC's "For Those About to Rock" with its cannon-fire opening bars. I felt a special soul connection to Joey. So has anyone who's ever known him.

Joey died on April 15, 2001, on Easter Sunday. At his funeral, Vin Scelsa gave the opening eulogy. The first DJ to break the Ramones on New York radio, he acknowledged Joey Ramone the legend, the front man of the band that ignited punk around the world. Mickey spoke of an older brother, of Jeffrey Ross Hyman, the man, and the shy, sickly boy the kids constantly picked on in school. Friends recounted how an early life of pain and humiliation was transformed by Joey's love of rock and roll and his relentless determination to overcome any obstacle. Rabbi Stephan Roberts described Joey Ramone as a deeply spiritual man who considered music a miracle of life.

A few weeks later, on May 19, 2001, we gathered at the Bowery Ballroom, at CBGB, at clubs and scenes everywhere to celebrate Joey's life and legacy on what would have been his fifty-first birthday. His brother Mickey has religiously kept the tradition of Joey's Birthday Bash every year since. Fans, punk luminaries, and friends gather to celebrate and further consecrate Joey's memory. After he died, Joey's mother, Charlotte, bought a country house in upstate New York. I recall standing with her one evening at sunset, watching from her deck as the colors turned from pink to blue. She had lost her second husband, Hank, in a car crash, survived a volatile first marriage, then cancer, and had recently lost her oldest child. She looked out across the mountains at the glorious setting sun, and with sheer exuberance exclaimed, "Donna, I love life!" Joey and Mickey got so much of their goodness, strength, and talent from her. Protective—lethal if you messed with her boys—Charlotte Lesher was the Great Mother Ramone.

Commando Johnny moved to Los Angeles shortly after I interviewed him in 1996. But something happened that day at the Empire Diner that changed my thinking about him. After we finished the interview, Johnny noticed my "Kill 'Em All and Let God Sort 'Em Out" T-shirt. I explained it was a gift from my dad: "Eighty-second Division Army Airborne, World War II combat veteran, *Calvados Commando*, he flew gliders in over the Rhine." Johnny's face opened up like a little kid; smiling, animated, he became a completely different person, started talking about how much he loved his father, how much he missed him. He pulled out a wallet photo of his dad, who had also served during the war. Johnny carried it with him, always. Johnny was an only child. "I need a lot of attention around the house," he laughed. Just then, a fan approached asking him for an autograph. Smiling, he signed it; gracious, like he was just starting out. The autograph was for a nine-year-old kid in dialysis. Ever grateful for the love and support of the fans, Johnny tended to the Ramones Mission like it was his baby, protecting it until his last breath.

In my interview with longtime Ramones insider George Seminara, he credits Johnny with defining and upholding what he calls the "Ramones Ideology." This supreme doctrine underscores both their Mission and Ministry. The Ramones, says Seminara, "were committed to representing all the kids who just barely got through high school, hung out, had dreams and hopes but no facility to get there." The Ramones Ideology poses a unique challenge: "Why learn how to play your instruments; just learn how to play your own songs."

According to Seminara, the Ramones Ideology also explains why there's such musical diversity in the punk genre—why, early on, everyone from Patti Smith to Devo, Blondie, and Talking Heads could represent it. But he suspects Johnny's rigor may have held the Ramones back professionally, stifling Dee Dee and Joey creatively. Above all, Johnny was afraid of isolating and betraying the fans, selling out, aborting the Mission and the Ministry. Upholding the Ramones Ideology meant the music had to stay the same, absolute and resolute.

Erich Fromm reminds us that creativity requires the courage to let go of certainties. While critics agree that the first four Ramones albums were brilliant, after that some complained the music had become redundant, says Seminara. But he disagrees, pointing out, for instance, that the band's subsequent experiments included synthesizers and bells on 1981's *Pleasant Dreams*. Ironically, "Warthog," Dee Dee's hard-driving nod to hardcore —a postpunk genre heavily influence by the Ramones—was viewed as too soft, even pop. On *Acid Eaters*, the Ramones 1993 cover album of '60s psychedelic garage tunes, the Who's Pete Townshend does backing vocals on "Substitute," and former porn star Traci Lords sings on "Somebody to Love." And then of course there's the Phil Spector project, *End of the Century*. Such "digressions" prompted the pious pricks to dismiss the Ramones as meanderers, philanderers, or worse: sellouts. In art, as in politics, this is why we can't have nice things!

On social media, an anonymous Ramones fan asked his friends, "Aside from Joey (of course) who is your next favorite Ramones?" Respondents admitted this was a tough one. Dee Dee was selected for his songwriting, Marky for generosity and friendliness to fans, and Johnny because he worked two times harder than he really had to. Every Ramones fan has his or her own personal Ramone, sort of like a personal savior: Tommy's the gifted visionary reminding talented kids that if they work hard, then following their dream is no cliché. Dee Dee's the outcast's outcast, a home for the displaced psyche or the motherless child, a vagabond artist on the astral plane. Joey's the wounded healer, the patron saint of lonely kids, even now—some say he's their only friend. As I wrote in his obituary for the *Village Voice*, Johnny's army is all the angry fatherless boys, disposable heroes who work hard, fight wars, and never get anything. Johnny's their captain; he'd never leave a soldier for dead, never betray the trust. For some fans, Johnny is the Father Ramone.

Joey was my dear friend, and I cherish the gifts Tommy, Mark, John, and C.J. so generously bestowed. But I was a Ramones fan first, and Dee Dee was my Ramone. The "personal" relationship between a fan and a beloved band member is a different sort of friendship, closer to what Erich Fromm describes in *The Art of Loving* as a human ideal, much more than a crush or groupie fixation, especially for Ramones fans. This connection is emotional and spiritual; it stands worlds apart from actual personal interaction and resides in the realm of faith, not of the material world but of a higher power.

For a long time I dressed like Dee Dee, lean and mean in a skimpy black leather jacket, skuzzy shredded jeans, Keds, a shredded T-shirt—action street wear, Queens style. I cut my hair in a bowl, straight and shiny like his. I sang his lyrics alone in my car like they came from my own heart, because they did. As a young, aspiring, cross-addicted sociologist, I sat fidgeting through graduate school seminars making up names for imaginary punk bands. I had to be sedated for the statistics final, and even then I couldn't relax, so I recited Dee Dee's lyrics silently to myself like a prayer . . . then I took my razor blade.

While the ferocious intensity of each Ramone exploded into the glorious whole we know and love, Dee Dee was the undisputed nuclear core of the Ramones, the true genius whose demonic wit formed the centerpiece of the Most American Band Ever. Wherever he was and whenever I saw him, Dee Dee opened up the world with childlike joy and wonder. On September 18, 2017, in what would have been Dee Dee's sixty-sixth birthday, some sixteen years after he died, tributes poured in all over social media. Former friends, fans, and associates honoring Dee Dee as a good guy, a little crazy but with a great heart; someone who is dearly missed. Describing him as a complicated, interesting man—at his worst and at his best—and one of the most important artists of our lifetime, one mourner reflected on how much smarter Dee Dee was than anyone knew. Fans remembered how Dee Dee hung around with them after shows, sharing humor and a love of rock and roll. According to Johnny Angel Wendell, "He was truly a bizarre character with too many personalities to keep track of. But he could knock out a song with amazing ease and given his generally tortured state of mind, that he lived as long as he did was not that bad."

Others recalled seeing Dee Dee at the Ritz, out of his mind

on something, a woman on each arm. They dubbed him the Lennon-McCartney of the Ramones, noting that he did it all on his own. George Seminara describes Dee Dee as a creative genius with multiple personalities, or at least an extreme bipolar disorder. "Meeting Dee Dee, you never knew who was gonna show up," he says.

Punk Avenue author and Senders' vocalist Phil Marcade places Dee Dee's talent up there with Brian Wilson of the Beach Boys. In his introduction to Dee Dee's memoir, *Lobotomy*, Legs McNeil describes him as "the last breed of authentic rock star, an authentic bad guy who 'got over.' An archetypal fuck up whose life was a living disaster, a male prostitute, would-be mugger, heroin dealer, an accomplice to armed robbery, and a genius poet who was headed to prison or an early grave. But was side-tracked by rock & roll."

According to George Seminara, Tommy was the only founding Ramone who could actually cook his own meals, rent an apartment, or drive a car for himself—the only adult among a crew of man-boys. Credited with creating their look, recognizing their talents, convincing the band to take the plunge, Tommy spent much of his life promoting, writing, performing, producing, and managing this infamous herd of cats. He wrote punk's most charming love song, "I Wanna Be Your Boyfriend," and most of "Blitzkrieg Bop." Without Tommy, there would have been no Ramones. He produced their albums when the less functional members couldn't quite show up. "They would come in and do the basic tracks and the vocals, and then I wouldn't see them for a month or two," Tommy told *Pitchfork*.

The Ramones' first three albums broke the sound barrier of

rock and roll, but in 2005 Tommy told the *Guardian* that after *Rocket to Russia* he was done, burned out from all the drama and infighting. "Johnny was getting more and more power, becoming harsher and harsher . . . he could be really mean, and he was good at getting the other guys to side with him." By the time the Ramones were given a Lifetime Achievement Award at the 2011 Grammys, Tommy was the sole surviving founding member.

As we know, early in his career as a recording engineer Tommy had worked on Jimi Hendrix's *Band of Gypsys*. In addition to the Ramones, Tommy produced bands like the Replacements, Talking Heads, and Redd Kross. In 2005, with his longtime partner, Claudia Tiernan, of the Simplistics, Tommy started playing bluegrass and country—guitar, dobro, banjo, and mandolin—forming Uncle Monk, an acoustic bluegrass folk duo. After studying for several years, Tommy became an impressive bluegrass vocalist and musician, and of this unlikely affinity he says: "There are a lot of similarities between punk and old-time music. Both are home-brewed music."

Since Johnny was a rhythm guitarist opposed on punk principle to leads, it was Tommy who filled in the leads, with Ed Stasium, Daniel Rey, or Walter Lure. In 2012, before he passed away, Tommy told Finnish journalist Jari-Pekka Laitio-Ramone that he and Claudia were working on a second Uncle Monk album. The first had been released in 2006. Tommy described the new album. "We keep coming up with new songs so we keep recording. Our new record will have some unique songs . . . mostly based on our lives and philosophies. There will be indie songs, bluegrass songs, old-time songs, romantic songs, and unclassifiable songs."

The building in Budapest where Tommy's family lived when he was born is now marked with a memorial written in Hungarian and English. It commemorates Tommy's birthplace and his contributions to music. The refugee from the Nazis and then the Commies is, to date, the only artist of Hungarian heritage to have been inducted into the Rock and Roll Hall of Fame. Tommy never stopped supporting and enhancing the efforts of others, and his passing marked the end of an era.

....

The early days of punk were seriously *guyville*. The boys bullied everything: the turntable, the stage, the pit. Even the great panel of luminaries who assembled onstage at CBGB as part of our 2005 effort to save the club was 100 percent male. Yes, Ellen Willis had warned us about punk's creeping misogyny. But ultimately it would be punk music that opened the door for girls to jump in, pick up guitars, play bass, drums, sing, and be nasty. *No more nice girls.*

The Ramones—especially Joey—would become inspirational figures for a new generation of female musicians. "I first heard the Ramones in the mid-'90s as a feminist riot-grrrl-loving teenager in Hollywood just starting to hone my voice. The band's song 'Sheena Is a Punk Rocker'—from its '50s throwback feel to its lyrics about female rebellion and escaping to New York City —inspired me to play and sing fast, raw, and loud," says Gen X writer and musician Solvej Schou in our interview. "Soon after, I moved to NYC for college, and soaked in the pop and grit that the Ramones brought to that city, and places like CBGB, where I would hang out (and see Joey Ramone play before he died)."

"To me," says Solvej, "Joey Ramone wasn't macho, even though he was a part of punk's revered coterie of male musicians, along with the Sex Pistols. He looked like a gangly girl-group delinquent in black leather, and was also geeky and Jewish, like me. That was a revelation. You could be awkward, Jewish, and scrappy and make primal, catchy music that stuck to eardrums like glue. It's no wonder that the band Sleater-Kinney name-drops Joey Ramone in its riot-grrrl sexual gender-flip anthem 'I Want to Be Your Joey Ramone' on its 1996 breakthrough album, *Call the Doctor*. Though drenching her words in irony, singer Corin Tucker belts about wanting to be idolized the way Joey Ramone was. And he was."

Although the New York Dolls, punk's first transsexual rock star Wayne/Jayne County, and Debbie Harry featured a gender-fluid post-girl-group-rocker "slut look," replete with garter belts, fishnet stockings, heavy liner, bleached-out hair piled eight miles high, vinyl miniskirts, gobs of lipstick, and spike heels, the typical nonurban female Ramones fans looked more like the band itself—like Pretenders' Chrissie Hynde or the Runaways' Joan Jett. In the early days, the Runaways had toured with their contemporaries, the Ramones. Johnny dismissed the influential LA-based all-girl band as a "bunch of dykes," while Dee Dee loved hanging out with them, and Joey remained friends with Joan for life.

The Ramones' music of course addressed the typical ups and downs of youthful relationships, drama, longing, betrayal, resentment, and heartbreak. "He's Gonna Kill That Girl" is a domestic-violence red flag. In their songs, men and women are equally annoying. "Tomorrow She Goes Away" can refer to your insufferable lover, houseguest, mother, or boss. "Judy Is a Punk" and "Sheena" are badass depictions of proactive women of the world out there taking risks—diehard music fans, in it for themselves. In their younger years, Johnny and Dee Dee were assholes to the women in their lives. Dating cross-addicted Joey would have been a full-time job. But in the 1990s the Ramones loomed heroic for a new radical feminist music subculture—riot grrrl.

A generation of feisty, smart, strong women and Generation X fans was born around the time the Ramones began spreading the word. The riot grrrl movement of the early 1990s meant women were taking music and meaning back. No longer would they measure their success, looks, bodies, or musical styles by established male standards. Instead of love stories and body hatred, ranting in confessional personal-political zines and songs, they were pissed off, ready to rumble, hurling venom and tampons from the stage.

Robin Mapes Tomlinson is a major Bikini Kill fan born on the East End of Long Island in 1980. The visual artist and mother of two now reflects: "The Ramones have done so much for music, especially for the bands that I listened to during my formative years. Without them we probably wouldn't have had the Pixies, Nirvana, or a large number of other influential bands that followed their lead. What they brought to riot grrrl in particular was the DIY mentality. Just picking up instruments and learning how to play them, not giving a fuck, and singing about things that were real."

Music journalist Jeanne Fury grew up in Jersey, what she calls "the land of Springsteen and Bon Jovi." Born in 1978, Fury says her earliest observations of male rock bands was this: "They were really good-looking and/or they were virtuosos. The Ramones were neither, and I love them deeply for it. Punk incarnate, they inadvertently gave everyone (including girls) license to be anything. This was more than a revelation for me—it was also a huge relief. You don't need to be pretty or perfect; you just need to have the guts to show up and throw down."

Journalism professor Evelyn McDonnell has written extensively on the Runaways and Björk and in 1995 coedited *Rock She Wrote* with Ann Powers, a groundbreaking collection of essays by women music writers. McDonnell summarizes the Ramones' impact on women in music: "The Ramones provided a bridge between the Girl Groups and riot grrrl, second-wave feminism and third—the Shirelles and the Donnas. They copped the aesthetic of the Ronettes and the Shangri-Las, inspired by women's bonds, beats, and bangs more than by the Beatles or other boy bands. And the simplicity of the Ramones' music embodied the DIY notion of punk; they democratized musicianship, opening doors for women. By singing about male prostitution and glue-sniffing, the Ramones promoted a kind of masculinity that was nonthreatening and sympathetic to feminine modes."

Punk meant owning the music, anger, power, and freedom. The Ramones had put a slight crack in patriarchy, and the rowdy girls came smashing through the end of the century. In addition to the male-scene dominance and the latent misogyny that troubled Ellen Willis, early punk's ethic of inclusion was further undermined by its sheer whiteness. The Ramones' fan base remains international and multiethnic, but with a few notable exceptions black fans and artists were barely visible in the early years of American punk. Marginalized as young people of color in a white scene, and viewed as race traitors in traditionally black music scenes, the Afropunk movement continues to challenge the norms of both white and black music subcultures.

Interviewed for "The Very Black History of Punk" video, musician and organizer Shawna Shante told Al Jazeera Media Network's Sana Saeed that pushed to the margins, banned from the mainstream, black performers have always been DIY. Booking their own shows, setting up tours through underground networks, "It doesn't get more punk rock than that." According to Afropunk activists, when you're black, you're "punk rock without even trying." As social outcasts, they explain, black people are "targets all the time." Unlike white punks, who can shave a Mohawk, cover a tattoo, remove a piercing, or change their clothes, black people can't opt out. They cannot remove their skin color.

By the early twenty-first century, Afropunk coalesced around bands like Death, Bad Brains, Suicidal Tendencies, Dead Kennedys, Fishbone, and Wesley Willis Fiasco. Further solidified by James Spooner's 2003 documentary, *Afropunk*, the Brooklyn-based Afropunk Music Festival established in 2005 by Spooner and Matthew Morgan continues to define and enrich Afropunk's unique cultural space, now expanding across the globe from Paris to Johannesburg. In recent years, Commodore Barry Park in Brooklyn has hosted upwards of sixty thousand Afropunk festivalgoers.

According to the *Huffington Post*, Afropunk is more than a festival; it's part of black culture, a place where the full diversity of lived black experience can find expression. Festivals include all ages, colors, shapes, and sizes. The festival website makes its

Donna Gaines

purpose clear: "Afro: as in, born of African spirit and heritage; see also black (not always), see also rhythm and color, see also other, see also underdog. Punk: as in, rebel, opposing the simple route, imbued with a DIY ethic, looking forward with simplicity, rawness and open curiosity; see also other, see also underdog." MSNBC reports, "Afropunk is pretty much one of the ultimate voices for young black free thinkers." The *New York Times* notes, "There's a reason the main stage was flanked by two giant flags, bearing that list of rules: No Sexism, No Racism, No Ableism, No Ageism, No Homophobia, No Fatphobia, No Transphobia, and finally, No Hatefulness." Afropunk is meant to be the ultimate inclusive space. In 2015, along with headliners Lauryn Hill, Grace Jones, and Lenny Kravitz was Marky Ramone, joining with Jillian Harvey of Lion Babe onstage at the two-day festival.

A visual artist and musician, Militia Vox is a key figure in the Afropunk scene. As an X-ennial, she's part of the microgeneration born between Gen X and the Millennials. "Truthfully," she says in our interview, "I think you'd be hard-pressed to find any part of alternative culture that has *not* been directly or indirectly influenced by the Ramones. Afropunk is no different. The ethos of punk rock is a mutual lifeblood. Plus, both hail from very New York energies. The power and direct simplicity of the Ramones is easily understood by this demographic, because of its outsider sound, look, and lyrics. It continues to speak thematically to the Afropunk movement because identity is everything in AP culture."

Vox adds, "I imagine that any black punk (Afropunk identified or not) would likely say that the Ramones were some part of their vital music history. When you're an underdog or marginalized, you hunt for art that you can relate to and that can speak to your story. The Ramones became champions for many because of this. I've definitely seen new and OG Afropunk bands that have taken words and musical ideas from the Ramones." For example, she says, the legendary Bad Brains took their name from a Ramones song, "Bad Brain," on the 1978 *Road to Ruin*— the first studio album, and the first one recorded with Marky on drums. A DC-based Rastafari band, Bad Brains are now considered pioneers of postpunk's hardcore music, though their sound incorporated elements of reggae, funk, hip-hop, and jazz. These sons and daughters of the Ramones are living proof that the band's Mission and Ministry—their dream of reclaiming rock and roll and engaging the marginal kids—is fulfilled. In addition to alternative, grunge, hardcore, queercore, and riot grrrl, the music and DIY ethics pioneered by the Ramones now infiltrate two spectacularly oppositional subcultures, cross-pollinating with both hip-hop and metal scenes in a movable feast. Locally and globally, the Ramones' impact is felt among the generations rising.

As a longtime music writer for the German fanzine *Slamzine*, Sebastian is a guitarist, songwriter, and singer who performed with such bands as Pitfall, Fuuukoh!, and more recently Kotzek. Born in 1981, Sebastian, like thousands of other kids coming of age in Germany in the late 1990s, was initially introduced to punk by bands like Green Day and Offspring. As Sebastian explains in our interview, the Ramones' music held the potential to get out the anger and frustration, "not only because it was very energetic and intense—especially the earlier Ramones songs —but also because it introduced humor and irony, addressing

'Nazi stuff' as modes of reflection and criticism." For example, he says, "think about the lyrics of 'Commando'; I can imagine this mind-set helped the postwar kids [his parents' generation] deal with their own parents' attitude towards the so-called Third Reich, which often included secrecy and denial."

Sebastian found out about the Ramones from a teacher who knew he liked punk. "I remember when my physics teacher, who was probably second-generation postwar introduced me to the Ramones. She gave me a tape with two Ramones albums and the song 'Commando' on it. So I guess this is a good example, if you want to show how important the Ramones are to that generation, when you have teachers passing around tapes with Ramones songs." The first time he heard "Blitzkrieg Bop," Sebastian says, "I was like, all right, now I get it! This was the stripped-down, straight-to-your-face version of the music big labels turned into some kind of business." Through his friendship with acclaimed Ramones photographer George DuBose, Sebastian says, "I also learned about New York City as a cultural 'melting pot' and center of the arts."

For German youth, says Sebastian, "I'm pretty sure that punk in general was very important as a way of rebelling against a system which reintroduced people who were Nazis during the so-called Third Reich to government and administration. This was a possibility to speak out against it, an art form to deny these practices and to cultivate something else."

Now a scholar, Dr. Sebastian reflects, "On a more abstract level, one could say that the Ramones are the reason for my interest in alternative aesthetics and sounds, DIY culture. All this research about older bands and especially the Ramones helped me to become a writer for music magazines." Today, as a young father living in the East German state of Saxony, Sebastian is shocked and angry over the recent victory of the far right in Germany's 2017 elections. "Again, we have 'nazis' in the parliament." For Sebastian, the emergence of an extreme right wing in German government is chilling. "We have an idiom, *Ich kann nicht so viel fressen wie ich kotzen möchte*, which can roughly be translated like this: 'I can't eat as much as I like to vomit.'" Although they are not in power in the state of Saxony, where Sebastian lives, he worries that the fascist AFD (Alternative for Germany) is now the strongest political force. "Poor Germany," he says, with deep sadness.

As authoritarian regimes and white supremacist groups rise worldwide, cultural resistance through music will continue to grow, attracting many more young people. Over the past four decades, the Ramones' music connected me to people like Sebastian and a network of kindred spirits around the world, fans and bands inspired by the Ramones who share similar core values, concerns, aesthetics, and sensibilities. International, crossing three generations, this lively web of affiliations also includes Mariano Asch of Argentina, who on Rockaway Records in 2005 released *Todos Somos Ramones*. The first worldwide Ramones tribute album, produced by Ed Stasium, with artists from Argentina, Brazil, Uruguay, Chile, the USA, Spain, Italy, France, England, Ireland, Japan, Belgium, and Germany contributing to the effort. When I visited Mexico in the late 1980s wearing a Ramones T-shirt, a nearby group of kids began shouting, "*Los Ramones!! Los Ramones!!*"

The Ramones' musical legacy is kept fresh by C.J., Marky, and

Richie Ramone, who continue to extend the Mission into a new century. Also sustaining it are celebratory events honoring the memories of Joey and Johnny in New York and Los Angeles respectively. In addition to Mickey's yearly birthday party for Joey, Linda Ramone presents an elegant annual tribute to Johnny Ramone at the Hollywood Forever Cemetery. The bronze statue Johnny designed of him playing guitar in his signature Ramones regalia has turned the site into a Ramones Mecca West. The tribute includes arts exhibits, cult films, horror movies, collectibles, and rock and roll—everything Johnny loved. Special guests have included Billy Idol, Vincent Gallo, and Steve Jones of the Sex Pistols. Dee Dee is also buried there, and in an act of intergenerational devotion, in 2017 the ashes of Soundgarden's Chris Cornell were buried twelve feet from Johnny's grave, marking the cemetery as hallowed ground for Ramones legions. From coast to coast, both events are fund-raisers for cancer research, to beat the disease that took out three of the four original Ramones. In galleries around the world, Dee Dee's artwork continues to be shown, along with Arturo's. Germany now has a Ramones museum. In Berlin!

The Ramones were the grand marshals leading a freaky parade with music we never imagined. After all the shows, the touring, the fans, books, documentaries, awards, toxic love affairs, family dramas, addictions, venomous in-fighting, chemotherapy, psychotherapy, scandals, vendettas, art, style, and ten million punk bands, in death the Ramones are finally getting their props. The Post-Ramones Empire now flourishes worldwide, more famous than ever before. *Time Has Come Today*. Welcoming people in from the margins means all access for every girl and boy, for people of all hues, any sexual orientation, nationality, or gender identity. This is what it means to be punk in the twenty-first century. *Los Ramones Ascensión!*

With no airplay, hit singles, platinum records, or proper respect in the land of their birth, outlasting most other contenders, never getting the recognition or remuneration they believed they deserved, the Ramones harbored a corrosive bitterness, frustration, and ultimately acceptance and resignation. A few weeks before he died, Joey appeared on the cover of *Spin*. For Joey, lying in a hospital bed, holding it in his hands, it meant everything.

Now exalted among artistic efforts, the Ramones' first album had piss-poor commercial success, zero airplay, and mixed reviews, peaking at a measly 111 on the US Billboard 200. "Rockaway Beach" got the highest charting in their career, at 66 in the Billboard 1000. Then, forty years after its release, *Ramones* was voted the greatest punk record of all times by *Rolling Stone*. In 2002, the same year the Ramones were inducted into the Rock and Roll Hall of Fame, *Spin* voted the Ramones *the greatest band ever*, second only to the Beatles. In 2011 the Ramones received a Grammy Lifetime Achievement Award. In 2014, thirty-eight years after its release, *Ramones* finally went gold, to which diehard fans replied, *Fuck you very much!*

On any given day, you'll hear the Ramones on rotation at my local skate park, where seven-year-old sk8terpunk Ryden surfs the wild concrete waves to "Blitzkrieg Bop" on his Gen X surfer dad's iPhone. You'll hear it blasting from my office at school, where my music studies students explore the Ramones' artistic process, the sacred relationship between the band and the fans, and punk as a critical form of protest music in history. Now more visible than ever, available at Target, Sears, and H&M, Ramones T-shirts for toddlers and grannies alike demonstrate the band's mass appeal. America's outsiders are now an American institution, an integral part of mass culture. On a daily basis we hear Ramones music rotating on TV commercials, in video cartoons, shows, and feature films. Nothing would have made them happier—this isn't the Ramones brand "selling out"; it's a belated victory parade for dedicated cultural combat veterans who fought a long war and accomplished their Mission, emerging triumphant.

Over forty years after the Ramones plotted to reclaim the airwaves, we can finally hear them on American radio! On Pandora, or college stations, introduced with reverence, tune into Marky Ramone's *Punk Rock Blitzkrieg* on Sirius XM's Faction Radio. The Ramones are honored daily on a multitude of websites around the world hosted by new fans and lifelong devotees alike. Now heralded as a game-changing moment in music history, *Ramones* places at number 33 in *Rolling Stone* magazine's list of the Top 500 Records Ever.

On the fortieth anniversary of *Ramones*, the *Observer*'s Tim Summers proclaimed the Ramones' debut album the best punk record of all times. "No 'mainstream' pop act had ever complimented the Ramones metronomic quality with guitars that never arpeggiated and basses that played only the tonic note of the chord, virtually without any variation. It all added up to something vastly unlike anything that had ever been heard before, yet vastly appealing." In the end, the Ramones seized the airwaves by changing the frequency.

In 2016, *Time Out* anointed the Ramones the best punk band ever. "Forget excess, pageantry or even practice—the threadbare efficiency of the Ramones' songwriting defined the punk spirit while they perfected a deftly ragged, inspirationally goofy and prodigiously catchy sound that few could equal, no matter how little they tried." The Sex Pistols took second place, then the Clash, Black Flag, and Dead Kennedys. With each anniversary of the Ramones' albums, critics, fans, and friends rejoice anew, and the legacy grows.

The Ramones left us with a road map, a blueprint, an instructional guide to living life creatively and with integrity. They dedicated their own lives to community building through subculture and style. Now uniformly credited with defining the punk genre, pinning it down, getting it out there, and staying true to form, the Ramones changed the way we think about music. They injected new life into old forms, reframed the old as the new, the familiar as cutting-edge.

As promised, they saved rock and roll, gave the outsiders a place to belong, modeled DIY ethics and practice, addressed the deep collective traumas we inherited from postwar parental generations—it was for American kids, and German kids too. They showed us the meaning of life and the secret to happiness: being true to who you are, no matter what. Now as never before, young people are learning how to resist and survive injustice and repression through oppositional subcultures and social movements. Older punks too are drawing on the spirit of rebellion that makes positive social change possible.

In 2012 Zack Furness published a collection of essays, interviews, reprinted studies, personal narratives, and advocacy

　　　　　　　Donna Gaines

tracts titled *Punkademics: The Basement Show in the Ivory Tower*. Following Dick Hebdige's groundbreaking 1978 work in *Subculture: The Meaning of Style*, a new generation of academics, remaining fascinated by "homemade 'zines and three chord songs," has found fertile ground in punk. In addition to studying it formally, theoretically—as a genre, subculture, or social movement —the contributors are committed to *practicing* punk values and ethics in their work as educators and scholars. Reflexively challenging the social relations of their own labor processes, they aim to humanize the alienating institutions the Ramones railed against. The Ramones embodied *theory and praxis* as a lifestyle, never imagining how their work might impact our lives, from the street to the towers of academe.

In one study, "Punk Rock Docs," the authors conclude that the new generation of professors has "beaten odds, shattered assumptions, jumped through the rigorous hoops of academia, been bestowed with the highest educational credentials and, in the end, might still somehow relate to the kid on the street corner with a spiked hairdo and black leather jacket. Joey Ramone, vocalist of punk rock pioneers, the Ramones, once sang the line, 'Gonna get my PhD' in the band's 1977 song, 'Teenage Lobotomy.'" As the authors note, "Joey Ramone never did attain such level of education before his passing in 2001. But at least his ambitions—like those of our participant population—were definitely couched in the right place." The social and cultural distance between academics and the people they purport to serve has troubled sociologists from C. W. Mills to Alvin Gouldner and also Paulo Freire. The Ramones taught me something about doing sociology too.

Following Dee Dee's mandate that rock and roll should be simple—"three words and a chorus, and the three words should be good enough to say it all"—I hoped early on to apply this to the study of the social world, to reclaim the rock-and-roll heart that had once been sociology, the "Queen of the Sciences." The Ramones are partially responsible for my career choices. Ever implied in the promise of upward mobility—the move "up class" —is the severing of old ties. Thanks to the Ramones, I never lost my Queens roots (or my accent). The Ramones' fresh DIY spirit lives in everything I care about—from writing and teaching to home repairs, gardening, art, dancing, bodysurfing, even spirituality. In the Ramones, I too found something to believe in. I place the Ramones among my great mentors.

Sometimes rock stars, like authors or actors, can be jerks. But the Ramones were true blue, neither posers nor imposters. They personified American punk, the City of New York, the 1970s, oppositional youth subculture, and the human struggle itself— triumph, tragedy, and truth. They helped me make better sense of myself, my own biography in history, life at a particular moment in time.

Legs McNeil explained the naming of *Punk Magazine*, and the social origins of the term itself, to Jon Savage. "On TV, if you watched cop shows, when the cops finally catch the mass murderer, they'd say 'you dirty punk.' It was what your teachers would call you. It meant that you were the lowest." In punk, says McNeil, "all of us dropouts and fuck-ups got together and started a movement. We'd been told all our lives that we'd never amount to anything. We're the people who fell through the cracks of the educational system."

The Ramones Ideology began in the 1970s on the streets of Forest Hills, in their own teenage wasteland. George Seminara described Johnny's "Ramones Ideology" as the band's commitment to "the aimless high school kids in the 1970's," kids "like the heavy metal fans of the 1980's." By the late 1980s, punk sensibilities of refusal and DIY had infiltrated metal music to create a hybrid form known as thrash, ruled by Metallica, Anthrax, and Megadeth.

One difference between the practice of journalism and doing sociology has to do with time. The journalist must seize the moment, identify and describe what's happening, show how it relates to us, to the zeitgeist. The sociologist lurks in the shadows, quietly watching, gathering evidence. It's still too soon to grasp the full measure of the Ramones' legacy. The Ramones are a punk's definition of true kingship; in Celtic mythology the king willingly returns his body to the soil in order to fertilize his culture. And so they did.

The good, the bad, and the ugly. The Beatles sparked an everlasting revolution in music, style, values, and subculture in the 1960s. The Ramones had a dream to be America's Beatles, to have a profound impact on music. "They were the Bizarro World Beatles," *Ramones* producer Craig Leon told the *Observer*. Or, as *Rolling Stone*'s Michael Gilmore eulogized with rueful tenderness, "The Ramones changed the world and then they died."

Yes, the corner of gentrified East Second Street and the Bowery is now *Joey Ramone Place*, reclaiming the sanctity of CBGB, immortalizing the relationship between the King of Punk and the city that spawned him. It's the most frequently stolen street sign in New York City. Next to Forest Hills High School is another street sign, *Ramones Way*. A marginalized band of misfits for marginalized misfit kids, unkempt, untrained, unprepared, the Ramones are finally being recognized as great *musicians*, skilled innovators of punk's sound and style. Now acknowledged for their moral authority as the embodiment of DIY, punk ethics, values, and norms, the Ramones are vindicated. As Commando Johnny said, "Maybe everyone does love you when you're dead."

To their deep frustration as artists, the Ramones believed that they never got their just rewards. Tragically, glory came after they died. Except for their fans, a multitude of new bands they inspired, and several enlightened critics, for most of their time on earth, as their biographers have argued, the Ramones felt undervalued and ignored in America. Their US sales, airplay, charting, and exposure never approached their prowess globally. Yet they are our Ramones, a loyal, steadfast, hardworking American band who reclaimed rock and roll, kick-started a new musical genre, punk as praise music of American popular culture. The Ramones gave us everything they had. Their well-known grueling touring schedule—2,263 shows from 1974 to 1996, trapped in a smelly van with assigned seats, power trips, and toxic relationships, eating junk food, sleeping in crappy motel rooms over some 761,405 miles—was born of economic necessity as well as idealism; they couldn't make a living off their record sales. In the end, it wore them down spiritually, emotionally, and physically. *And he said, "Truly, I say to you, no prophet is acceptable in his hometown"*—Luke 4:24.

Anointed ultimately as the Gods of Punk, the Ramones of New York revolutionized popular culture at the core. The Ramones lived to play, and played to live; their synergy with the audience was as much a part of the music as the composition and performance. Only hip-hop engages audiences with such passion. Da bruddahs have given us many brilliant anthems to hang our dreams on. Whether by land or by sea, the Ramones never forgot their primary purpose: to be true to their fans. When they played, they did it for us. They never wavered, never betrayed our faith. Their impact on popular music, their influence on youth subculture, cannot be measured in the cold, banal, quantitative language of market shares, chart positions, and radio airplay. No true punk gives a shit what those assholes think anyway.

In the beginning the Ramones would walk onstage to a military drum roll. By the middle of the 1980s, the Ramones kicked off each show with "The Good, the Bad and the Ugly," the opening theme from Sergio Leone's 1966 Spaghetti Western opus starring Clint Eastwood. Once you heard that music, tingles and shivers traveled down your spine. That music primed the fans, and oh what I would give to see it now. After six live, fourteen studio, and twelve compilation albums, seventy-seven singles, several tribute albums, 2,263 shows, and twenty-two years of hard touring, on August 6, 1996, the Ramones played their last show at the Palace Ballroom in Hollywood, Los Angeles. It was Johnny's idea to close in LA. And there the Ramones effectively passed the torch to the next generation of young musicians, the bands they had spawned. Assorted members of Rancid, Soundgarden, Pearl Jam, and Lemmy of Motörhead came onstage to honor the Ramones.

That night, after several encores, the Ramones walked off the stage forever. Music from the *Good, the Bad and the Ugly* returned. But this time it was the main theme, "Ecstasy of Gold." The Ramones were saying goodbye. "Ecstasy of Gold" bookended their career, handed the Mission over to the next generation. Metallica's Kirk Hammett was one of Johnny's closest friends; they bonded over a shared love of movie posters, especially old horror films. As a kid, the guitarist was deeply influenced by Johnny's forceful guitar work. "Ecstasy of Gold" is Metallica's opening theme music. That night, the song signified the Ramones' growth over a lifetime, their journey from lost, invisible, marginal boys to honorable men of great wisdom, talent, and stature. It's so beautiful, so powerful to witness that sometimes I can't bear to listen, even now.

I remember you. Like the proud-standing Militia of Lexington that fired the shot that sparked the American Revolution, the Ramones of New York City changed history. They continue to challenge us, asking us to consider who we really are, what we value, and what matters. As Ralph Waldo Emerson said, "To be yourself in a world that is constantly trying to make you something else is the greatest accomplishment." Even if you're the Ramones' mascot, Zippy the Pinhead, a dunce with a deformed cranium, you still belong.

In an era of lethal climate changes—storms, fires, and droughts—identity theft, hacked elections, open-fire massacres, American Nazi marches, terrorism at home and abroad, corruption, treason, increasing hatred and street violence against minorities and women, xenophobia, bullying, mass migration, campus rape, rape camps, and "animal Auschwitz" factory farming, sometimes life feels like it's war all the time, the Age of Trauma. One of the problems young people face is the inability to articulate or name what they feel. The Ramones opened the doors for any kid who has something to say.

The filmmaker Jordan Peele broke new ground with *Get Out*, his 2017 social horror movie about "casual racism." Here the monster is racism itself. "This film is how racism *feels*," lead actor Daniel Kaluuya told Los Angeles reporter Jen Yamato. "You get paranoid and you can't talk about it. You can't voice it. No one around you gets it, so you can't speak about it. And in the end it just comes out in a rage." As Peele explains, part of being black or a minority in this country is about distorted perception—the mind fuck of perceiving things you're told you are not perceiving. This, he says, is a state of mind. "It's a piece of the condition of being African American, certainly, that people may not know. They may not realize the toll that it does take—even if the toll is making us doubt ourselves." Art is the first line of resistance for deeply buried, vague, indefinable feelings. Music allows expression in positive and constructive ways that won't kill us or anyone else; it unites us in dissent and redeems us too. The Ramones told us so in ten thousand different ways.

Tommy offers his own thoughts on why the Ramones matter, in a 1976 quote from the band's official Twitter account. Noting that "New York was the perfect place to grow up neurotic," he says, "One of the reasons that the Ramones were so unique and original was that they were four original, unique people." Individuality, quirks, creative genius, originality, and dysfunction, everything our institutions (and socialization) try to beat out of us, the Ramones replenish.

Today the Ramones rule the airwaves, though not the way they imagined. Now rotated several times a day on TV commercials around the world, "Blitzkrieg Bop" began as the battle cry for the Ramones Mission. But 1987's more obscure "I Wanna Live" by Dee Dee and Daniel Rey may be their epitaph. No matter how grand we are, even a prince decked out in diamonds, we're still vulnerable, terrified of being exposed, still facing enemies real and imagined. From the end of the century to the start of another the Ramones remind us, *Don't give up*. Stand up, suit up, and show up for your life—for the good, the bad, and the ugly. It's important to give what you've got, do what you need to, to live. What does it mean today for a young person to say, "I want to live my life"?

Gabba Gabba Hey! As it was in the beginning, is now, and will be forever, at any age, in any language, the Ramones' words of welcome have become the standard greeting among fans, an invitation to the stranger to join in, to engage, to be part of. In 2016, long after our Ramones had exited the stage and this world, a young fan named Zax Reds described them as "the hardest working band, toured their lives away." They did that for us and they will be there for us wherever we roam, across the miles, the maps, and the years. Bell Spencer, a Millennial living halfway across the world, says, "Ramones feels alive to the fans. Ramones are never gonna stop."

ACKNOWLEDGMENTS

....

An award from Empire State College of the State University of New York's Faculty Development Fund Committee provided essential resources for this research. The Office of Academic Affairs graciously supported this project through a two-month reassignment leave. To Frank VanderValk, Alan Mandell, Terri Hilton, Janay Jackson, and my wonderful, dedicated colleagues and friends at the Old Westbury Unit and across the College, thank you for your continuous inspiration and support. To all my students past and present, you make it matter so much more.

Portions of this work were previously published in *A Misfit's Manifesto*, the *Village Voice*, *Spin*, and the essay for the Ramones' 2002 induction into the Rock and Roll Hall of Fame; also on my website, www.donnagaines.com. My interviews with Joey and Dee Dee appear in *End of the Century*. Other materials are based on several years of conversations, interviews, and adventures with Ramones and friends.

To the people interviewed for this project, thank you for your time, care, and generosity: Fraser Ottenelli, Deena Weinstein, Tom Smucker, Alison Stone, Terri 805, Robin Mapes Tomlinson, Fred Fredman, Cynthia Mitchell, Sebastian Nathan, Robin Storey, Robert Holm, Jeanne Fury, Militia Vox, and Solvej Schou. Thanks too to Jonas Engelmann, Greil Marcus, Johnny Angel Wendell, George Seminara, George DuBose, George Tabb, C.J. Ramone, Jari-Pekka Laitio-Ramone, Monte A. Melnick, and Mickey Leigh for illuminating insights and a lifetime of good works. To the wonderful Evelyn McDonnell for suggesting this project; to Stephen Hull for his editorial insight, humor, and intuitive guidance, and to the terrific people at ForeEdge/UPNE; to Robert Christgau and all the *Village Voice* editors who schooled me, including Ann Powers, who invited me to interview the Ramones in 1996. Thanks to my agent, Susan Ramer, for her integrity and wisdom. All respect and gratitude to my great mentor, editor, and friend, the late Ellen Willis, forever the voice in my head admonishing, "You're overexplaining!!!!"

Special love to the Sullivan, Nafte, Holm, and Jalbert families, to Mary Anne Trasciatti, Mona More, Bob DiNapoli, Leila Kate, "The Club," and the ocean. To the blessed memories of the Rev. James Jeffrey, Lewis A. Coser, Charlotte Lesher, Johnny Bully, Billy Rogers, Lemmy, Anthony Bourdain, Johnny Cash, Johnny Thunders, Jerry Nolan, Jeff Hyman, Douglas Colvin, John Cummings, Tomas Erdily, and Arturo Vega. You made the world bigger, brighter, bolder, and better. *¡Para Los Ramoneros de Argentina, los verdaderos creyentes, llevan la fe!*

To my three favorite musicians: big band vocalist Betty Bradley (Mom), who taught me to love the world, the words, and the music. To DOM, Army Airborne, *salsero grande*, drummer, and tough-love dad, who taught me to stand my ground and stay the course. To my muse and junko partner since 1978, Raymond Jalbert. "If I know what love is, it's because of you."

Donna Gaines
www.donnagaines.com
donna@donnagaines.com

SOURCES

....

Books

Adorno, Theodor W., et al. *The Authoritarian Personality*. Vol. 1 in *Studies in Prejudice Series*. Harper & Row, 1950.

Alcoholics Anonymous: Big Book Reference Edition for Addiction Treatment. 2014.

Bangs, Lester, and Greil Marcus, eds. *Psychotic Reactions and Carburetor Dung: The Work of a Legendary Critic: Rock 'n' Roll as Literature and Literature as Rock 'n' Roll*. Anchor Books, 2003.

Beeber, Steven Lee. *The Heebie-Jeebies at CBGB's: A Secret History of Jewish Punk*. Chicago Review Press, 2006.

Berger, Bennett. *Looking for America: Essays on Youth, Suburbia, and Other American Obsessions*. Prentice-Hall, 1971.

Bessman, Jim. *Ramones: An American Band*. St. Martin's, 1993.

Bockris, Victor. *Beat Punks: New York's Underground Culture from the Beat Generation to the Punk Explosion*. Da Capo, 2000.

Brake, Michael. *The Sociology of Youth Culture and Youth Subcultures (Routledge Revivals): Sex and Drugs and Rock 'n' Roll?* Routledge, 2014.

Breggin, Peter. *Talking Back to Prozac: What Doctors Aren't Telling You about Today's Most Controversial Drug*. St Martin's Paperbacks, 1995.

Croteau, David, and William Hoynes. *Experience Sociology*, 3rd ed. McGraw-Hill Education, 2017.

Durkheim, Emile. *Suicide: A Study in Sociology*. Free Press, 1966.

Engelmann, Jonas. "*Luftmenschen*, Golems, and Jewish Punks: On the Pop Cultural Reflection of Jewish Identity in the Post-Shoah." In

141

Entangled Memories: Remembering the Holocaust in a Global Age, edited by Marius Henderson and Julia Lange. Winter Universität Verlag, 2017.

Eyerman, Ron. *Cultural Trauma: Slavery and the Formation of African American Identity*. Cambridge Cultural Social Studies. Cambridge University Press, 2002.

Fromm, Erich. *The Art of Loving*. Harper Perennial Modern Classics, 2006.

Furness, Zack, ed. *Punkademics*. AK Press, 2012.

Gaines, Donna. "Border Crossing in the U.S.A." In *Microphone Fiends: Youth Music and Youth Culture*, edited by Tricia Rose and Andrew Ross. Routledge, Chapman & Hall, 1994.

———. "The Local Economy of Suburban Scenes." In *Adolescents and Their Music*, edited by J. Epstein. Garland, 1994.

———. *A Misfit's Manifesto: The Sociological Memoir of a Rock & Roll Heart*. Rutgers University Press, 2007.

———. *Teenage Wasteland: Suburbia's Dead End Kids*. University of Chicago Press, 1998.

Gobello, Marcello. *Los Ramones: Demasiado Duros Para Morir* (in Spanish). Lenoir Libros, 2008.

Heylin, Clinton. *From the Velvets to the Voidoids: A Pre-Punk History for a Post-Punk World*. Penguin Group, 1993.

Holmstrom, John, and Bridget Hurd, eds. *Punk: The Best of Punk Magazine*. HarperCollins, 2012.

King, Vera Ramone. *Poisoned Heart: I Married Dee Dee Ramone (The Ramones Years)*. Phoenix, 2009.

Lattin, Don. *Distilled Spirits: Getting High, Then Sober, with a Famous Writer, a Forgotten Philosopher, and a Hopeless Drunk*. University of California Press, 2012.

Leigh, Mickey, with Legs McNeil. *I Slept with Joey Ramone: A Punk Rock Family Memoir*. Simon & Schuster, 2010.

Marcade, Phil. *Punk Avenue: Inside the New York City Underground 1972–1982*. Three Rooms, 2017.

McNeil, Legs, and Gillian McCain. *Please Kill Me: The Uncensored Oral History of Punk*. Grove, 1996.

Melnick, Monte A., and Frank Meyer. *On the Road with the Ramones*. Sanctuary Publishing, 2007.

Mills, C. W. *The Sociological Imagination*, 40th anniv. ed. Oxford University Press, 2000.

Nouwen, Henri. *The Wounded Healer: Ministry in Contemporary Society*. Image Books, 1979.

Popoff, Martin. *Ramones at 40*. Sterling, 2016.

Ramone, Dee Dee, with Veronica Kaufman. *Lobotomy: Surviving the Ramones*. Da Capo, 2000.

Ramone, Johnny. *Commando: The Autobiography of Johnny Ramone*. Abrams Image, 2012.

Ramone, Marky, with Richard Herschlag. *Punk Rock Blitzkrieg: My Life as a Ramone*. Touchstone, 2015.

Reynolds, Simon. *Shock and Awe: Glam Rock and Its Legacy from the Seventies to the Twenty-First Century*. Dey Street Books, 2016.

Sartre, Jean-Paul. *Existentialism and Humanism*. Methuen, 2007.

Savage, John. *England's Dreaming: Anarchy, Sex Pistols, Punk Rock and Beyond*. St. Martin's Griffin, 2002.

True, Everett. *Hey Ho Let's Go: The Story of the Ramones*. Omnibus, 2002.

Weinstein, Deena. *Heavy Metal: The Music and Its Culture*, rev. ed. Da Capo, 2000.

Willis, Ellen. *Out of the Vinyl Depths: Ellen Willis on Rock Music*, edited by Nona Willis Aronowitz. University of Minnesota Press, 2011.

Print and Electronic Articles

Anderson, Rick. "Ramones by Ramones Review." *Music Library Association*, Second Series, 58, no. 3 (March 2002): 657–58.

Bangs, Lester. "Free Jazz/Punk Rock." www.notbored.org/bangs.html.

———. "Iggy Pop: Cobo Arena, Detroit." *New Musical Express* 5. www .rocksbackpages.com/Library/Writer/lester-bangs/.

———. "The White Noise Supremacists." *Village Voice*, 1979.

Beinart, Peter. "The Rise of the Violent Left." www.theatlantic.com /magazine/archive/2017/09/the-rise-of-the-violent-left/534192/.

Betrock, Alan. R "We Play Music for People Who Don't Have a Lot of Time." Interview with Tommy Ramone, *Soho News*, 1975, available in www.theguardian.com/music/2013/apr/17/rocks-backpages -ramones-new-york-1975.

Blumenthal, Ralph. "Punk, and Jewish: Rockers Explore Identity." www.nytimes.com/2009/06/13/nyregion/13punk.html.

Campbell, Marc. "Hey Ho! The Ramones 'Blitzkrieg Bop' Deconstructed." http://dangerousminds.net/comments/hey_ho _the_ramones_blitzkrieg_bop_deconstructed.

"Chris Cornell Ashes Buried Next to Johnny Ramone." www.tmz .com/2017/05/26/chris-cornell-buried-next-to-johnny-ramone -hollywood-forever/.

Christgau, Robert. "*Ramones*." www.robertchristgau.com/get_artist .php?name=Ramones.

Coplan, Chris. "Ya Know?" https://consequenceofsound.net/2012/05 /album-review-joey-ramone-ya-know/.

"Critically Divisive Musicians: Exhibit A (Ramones)." https:// rockcritics.com/2008/04/11/critically-divisive-musicians-exhibit-a -ramones/.

"Did the Ramones Have Good Musicianship?" http://punk-music

.yoexpert.com/entertainment-artists-and-bands/did-the-ramones
-have-good-musicianship-49529.html.

Erlewine, Stephen Thomas. "*Ramones*." www.allmusic.com/album
/ramones-mw0000691207.

"40 Greatest Punk Albums of All Time." www.rollingstone.com
/music/lists/40-greatest-punk-albums-of-all-time-201604.

Freeman, Rob. "On Recording Ramones." http://titlewaveproductions
.com/uploads/RobFreeman_RecordingRamones.pdf.

Gaines, Donna. "End of the Century." *Village Voice*, 1996.

———. "The Great Mother Ramone: Charlotte Lesher 1926–2017."
www.punkglobe.com/motherramone.html.

———. "Johnny Ramone 1948–2004." *Village Voice*, 2004.

———. "Last Stand at CBGB's." *Village Voice*, 2005.

———. "Night Rally: Youth & Fascism Today." *Maximum RocknRoll*,
1986.

———. "Not 53rd and 3rd: Joey Ramone Gets His Place." *Village Voice*,
2003.

———. "Ramones." Induction, Rock and Roll Hall of Fame, Waldorf
Astoria, New York City, 2002.

———. "The Ramones, A Love Story." *Village Voice*, 1996.

———. "Ronnie Spector: She Talks to Rainbows." *Village Voice*, 1999.

———. "Too Tough to Die: Last Days of Joey Ramone." *Spin*, 2001.

Gilmore, Mikal. "The Curse of the Ramones." www.rollingstone.com
/music/features/the-curse-of-the-ramones-20160519.

Goncalo, Jack, and Barry Staw. "Individualism: Collectivism and
Group Creativity." www.haas.berkeley.edu/faculty/papers
/stawgoncalo.pdf.

Gregory, James. "The Last Ramone." https://pitchfork.com/features
/interview/6035-tommy-ramone/.

Helmore, Edward. "They Wanted to Be as Big as the Beatles: Revising

the Ramones Legacy." www.theguardian.com/music/2016/apr/08
/the-ramones-legacy-queens-museum-new-york-exhibit.

Huddle, Mark. "Interview: Cheetah Chrome of Rocket from the
Tombs and Dead Boys." www.verbicidemagazine.com/2010/07/27
/interview-cheetah-chrome/.

Huey, Steve. "Joey Ramone Bio." www.allmusic.com/artist/joey
-ramone-mn0000173487.

Hughes, Rob. "The Story behind the Song: Blitzkrieg Bop by the
Ramones." http://teamrock.com/feature/2014–07–14/story-behind
-the-song-blitzkrieg-bop-by-the-ramones.

Jacobson, Mark. "Anarchy in the USA vs. the U.K.: Legs McNeil and Jon
Savage, Present-at-the-Creation Punk Scholars, on the Spirit of '76."
http://nymag.com/news/features/legs-mcneil-jon-savage-2013–4/.

"Johnny Ramone." www.punkguitarists.com/johnny-ramone/.

Laitio-Ramone, Jari-Pekka. www.ramonesheaven.com/ramones.html.

Lamborn, Bill. "La Banda Punk Argentina: The Ramones
Phenomenon in Buenos Aires." www.staythirstymedia
.com/200806–022/html/200806-ramones-argentina.html.

Leland, John. "Bonzo Goes to Bitburg." *Spin*, 1985, "Singles," p. 39.

Marcus, Greil. https://greilmarcus.net/2014/07/10/ramones-loosen-up
-rocket-to-russia-12–12–77/.

Martinson, Jane. "The Virtues of Vice: How *Punk* Magazine Was
Transformed into a Media Giant." www.theguardian.com
/media/2015/jan/01/virtues-of-vice-magazine-transformed-into
-global-giant.

Marx, Wallace, Jr. "The Gear of the Original Punks." www
.premierguitar.com/articles/Maximum_Energy_The_Gear_of_
the_Original_Punks_?page=2.

McNeil, Legs. "Tommy Ramone: His Story as Told to Legs McNeil."
www.hollywoodreporter.com/news/tommy-ramone-his-story-as
-718469.

Merline, David. "How the Ramones Saved Rock-n-Roll." www
.web2carz.com/lifestyle/music/3426/how-the-ramones-saved
-rock-n-roll.

"The Ramones in the 80's." https://burningambulance.com/2014/12/12
/the-ramones-in-the-80s/.

"Readers Poll: The Best Ten Ramones Songs." www.rollingstone.com
/music/pictures/readers-poll-the-10-best-ramones-songs-20130717.

Roberts, Randall. "Tommy Ramone: The Drummer for the Ramones
Created an Essential Punk Rhythm." www.latimes.com
/entertainment/music/posts/la-et-ms-tommy-ramone-drummer
-for-the-ramones-created-an-essential-punk-rhythm-20140712
-story.html.

Rollins, Henry. "The Ramones Rescued Rock and Roll." www.laweekly
.com/music/henry-rollins-the-ramones-rescued-rock-and-roll
-4860578.

Rubin, Nick. "The Ramones." American National Biography Online,
February 2000. www.anb.org/articles/18/18–03904.html.

Scott, Carl Eric. "Carl's Rock Songbook No. 99: The Ramones as
Holocaust-Haunted Pop Art." www.nationalreview.com/blog
/postmodern-conservative/carls-rock-songbook-no-99-ramones
-holocaust-haunted-pop-art-carl-eric/.

Scott, William. "CJ Ramone: Had I Not Served in the USMC . . ."
www.punktastic.com/radar/cj-ramone-had-i-not-served-in-the
-usmc-id-have-drank-and-partied-until-i-was-dismissed-or-dead/.

Sisario, Ben. "'Ramones': The Story behind a Debut Album from Punk
Pioneers." www.nytimes.com/2016/03/19/arts/music/ramones-the
-story-behind-a-debut-album-from-punk-pioneers.html.

Sommer, Tim. "The Ramones Debut Album Is Still the Best Punk-
Record of All Time." http://observer.com/2016/04/the-ramones
-debut-album-is-still-the-best-punk-record-of-all-time/.

"*Spiegel* Interview with Mel Brooks: With Comedy, We Can Rob Hitler

of His Posthumous Power." www.spiegel.de/international/spiegel
/spiegel-interview-with-mel-brooks-with-comedy-we-can-rob-hitler
-of-his-posthumous-power-a-406268.html.

Stevens, Jane Ellen. "Addiction Doc Says: It's Not the Drugs; It's
the ACEs Adverse Childhood Experiences." https://acestoohigh
.com/2017/05/02/addiction-doc-says-stop-chasing-the-drug-focus
-on-aces-people-can-recover/.

Stratton, Jon. "Jews, Punk, and the Holocaust: From the Velvet
Underground to the Ramones: The Jewish-American Story."
Popular Music 24, no. 1 (January 2005): 79–105. www.jstorr.org
/stable/387759.

Sweeting, Adam. "Tommy Ramone Obituary." www.theguardian.com
/music/2014/jul/13/tommy-ramone.

Teather, David. "Maria Bartiromo: Money Honey Who Stirred
Ramones Hormones." www.theguardian.com/business/2006/
jul/14/3.

"Tommy Ramone, Drummer of Cultic Punk Rock Band the Ramones."
http://hungarytoday.hu/news/hungarian-roots-tommy-ramone
-drummer-cultic-punk-rock-band-ramones-68880.

White, Timothy. "The Importance of Being a Ramone." www
.rollingstone.com/music/news/the-importance-of-being-a-ramone
-19790208.

Wolk, Douglas. "I Wanna Be Joey." www.slate.com/articles/arts
/culturebox/2001/04/i_wanna_be_joey.html.

Wollcott, James. "The Last to Go." www.vanityfair.com/culture/2014
/07/the-last-to-go.

Wurster, Jon. "Drumming along with Tommy Ramone." www.spin
.com/2014/07/jon-wurster-remembers-tommy-ramone-rip/.

Yamato, Jen. "Jordan Peele on 'Get Out,' the Horror Film about Racism
That Obama Would Love." www.latimes.com/entertainment/

movies/la-et-get-out-jordan-peele-racism-horror-america-20170224
-story.html.

Yardley, William. "Arturo Vega: Shepherd for the Ramones Dies at 65."
www.nytimes.com/2013/06/12/arts/music/arturo-vega-spokesman
-and-designer-for-the-ramones-dies-at-65.html.

Films and DVDs

Danny Says. Brendon Toller, dir. (2015).

End of the Century: The Story of the Ramones. Dim Fields, dir. (2003).

Ramones. Rhino Records Warner Strategic Marketing, Sire (2001).

The Ramones: It's Alive 1974–1996. George Seminara, dir. (2007).

Ramones Leave Home. Rhino Records Warner Strategic Marketing,
Sire (2001).

Ramones Raw. John Cafiero, dir. (2004).

Todos Somos Ramones. Rockaway Records, Buenos Aires (2005).

"The Very Black History of Punk Music" with Sana Saeed, Al Jazeera
Media Network. www.youtube.com/watch?v=WgIWDZ1xxdM
(n.d.).

Websites

Diffuser.fm.the-ramones-last-show-anniversary/

http://www.donnagaines.com/shrine/shrine2.htm#CBGB

http://www.donnagaines.com/shrine/shrine2.htm#Dee_Dee_Ramone

http://www.donnagaines.com/shrine/shrine2.htm#Joey_Ramone

http://www.donnagaines.com/shrine/shrine2.htm#Johnny_Ramone

http://www.george-dubose.com

https://www.ramones.com

http://www.ramonesheaven.com/ramones.html

https://www.ramonesmuseum.com
https://www.songkick.com/artists/99871-ramones
https://twitter.com/RamonesOfficial

Author Interviews

January–October 2017: Sebastian Nathan, Raymond Jalbert, Jeanne
Fury, Robin Mapes Tomlinson, Robin Storey, Cynthis Mitchell,
Johnny Angel Wendall, Evelyn McDonnell, Alison Stone, Terri
805, Solvej Shou, Fred Fredman, Jari-Pekka Laitio-Ramone, C.J.
Ramone, Monte A. Melnick, Mickey Leigh, George Seminara, and
Militia Vox.